283.09
HUG
1558

Hughes, L
st. georg
episcopal church

DATE DUE

ST. GEORGE'S EPISCOPAL CHURCH
GERMANTOWN, TENNESSEE

The First Twenty Years

By
Leonard V. Hughes, Jr.

Edited By
James D. Russell

First Edition

Published By
The Rector, Wardens and Vestry of
St. George's Episcopal Church
June, 1984

CALVARY EPISCOPAL CHURCH
102 N. SECOND
MEMPHIS, TENNESSEE

© 1984 by St. George's Episcopal Church, Germantown, Tennessee; Leonard V. Hughes, Jr.:

All rights reserved, including rights of reproductions and use in any form or by any means, including the making of copies by any photo process, or by any electronic or mechanical device, printed or written or oral, or recording for sound or visual reproduction or for use in any knowledge or retrieval system or device, unless permission in writing is obtained from the copyright proprietors.

Printed and bound in the United States of America

International Standard Book Number: 0-9613533-0-9

Library of Congress Catalog Card Number: 83-50804

St. George's Episcopal Church
P.O. Box 38447 8250 Highway 72
Germantown, Tennessee
38138-0447

Dedicated to the Glory of

God and in Memory of

John Bridges Scruggs
John Bell Hebron
Hiram Tyre Adair
Mary Ellen Graves
Dorothy G. Walker Kirby
Joseph Abram Martin
Geraldine Apperson Martin
Marie (Mamie) Theresia Cloyes
The Reverend Charles Leonidas Widney
The Reverend Thomas Adams Roberts
and in honor of
Lotta Lee Yancey Adair
Carl Richmond Graves

ACKNOWLEDGEMENTS

Many individuals supported the author's task of collecting materials and photographs for this book as well as sharing in its composition. Their contributions are gratefully credited here as follows:

Photographic Editor - Shirley Warfield

Research and Composition - Carol Ann Rockett
                          Barbara Apperson

Cover - James D. Randolph, Jr.

Research - Kenneth W. Robertson, Louise F. Rosengarten, Ednamae Thompson, Dorothy Kirby Wills, Lotta Adair, Kathyn Zook, Nora Holden Kellerhals, Helen O'Brien, Dorothy Robertson, Otto Lyons, Nadine Lyons, Betty McCall, Judge Carl Graves, Isabelle Scruggs Wade, Elizabeth Anderson, Harry F. Cloyes, Nancy Sutton, Ann Randolph, S. Caya Phillips, Denise P. Hughes, the Reverend Canon George Fox, Marion Dubose, Jonell Martin;

To my wife, Denise, and the Reverend Allen Cooke for their constant support and encouragement;

To my law partners, John L. McWhorter and Lester T. Wener, for their support and my secretary, Jeanine Givens, for manuscript preparation.

Contents

Preface

The Pre-Mission Story   1

The Founders   21

The Mission Years   59

The Early Parish   89

A New Beginning   98

Epilogue   116

Appendix:

    Episcopal Churchwomen   1

    Organists and Choir   9

    Priests and Rectors   14

    Vestry Officers   15

    Church School Officers and Attendance   21

    Layreaders and Chalicebearers   22

    Growth Through the Years   25

    Sources and Bibliography   27

    Historical Document Index   33

    Historical Documents

    Index

ERRATA

"St. George's Episcopal Church, Germantown, Tennessee-
The First Twenty Years"

Pages 4, 13, 17, 34, 54, 64, 84 and Index:
Where mentioned in the text or referenced in the footnotes, the name "Ellen Davies-Rogers" or "Rogers", same should appear "Ellen Davies-Rodgers" and "Rodgers".

Page 5   In the seventh line the word "....several" should be "seven".

Page 6   The photograph which appears is that of The Reverend George White, seventh Rector of Calvary Church, Memphis, 1859-1883. A photograph of The Reverend Prentice Pugh appears below.

The Reverend Prentice Pugh

Preface

When this effort began a little more than two years ago, it was to be a definitive story of St. George's as a mission and parish covering the entire fifty years of its existence. It soon became quite clear to the author that the time allotted to produce such a chronicle was not adequate if it were to be published in St. George's fiftieth anniversary year. The decision was made to publish a detailed story of the first twenty years to assure for the future our heritage would not be lost. As the reader will observe, the story begins well before the organization of St. George's as a mission, in fact, more than fifty years prior to that event. The reader will also note that the first twenty years is a logical historical point at which to divide the story within the fifty year history of the parish.

It has been said that without vestry minutes the production of an Episcopal church history is an unsurmountable task. The author has, nevertheless, forged ahead, perhaps failing to understand it could not be done. The reader must make the final decision keeping in mind that vestry minutes existed for only the last six of the twenty year period.

To Calvin Warfield goes the credit for the suggestion of an epilogue as an appropriate addition to the publication on the parish's fiftieth anniversary. Having obvious merit, an epilogue has been included without footnotes or authorities, however, the same care as to accuracy was exercised as with the preceding text.

A church history should be more than a mere chronology of events and experiences in the birth and growth of a parish. It should be a factual account of flesh and blood people who have fulfilled their ministry through corporate desire and effort. With the generous help of many we who are responsible for this volume have made a humble attempt to revive the spirit of those who, propelled by an obvious sense of purpose, struggled to establish and nurture the church that is now St. George's. Hopefully, some brave soul will find the time, enthusiasm and perseverence to continue this story to its fifty year conclusion.

                        Leonard V. Hughes, Jr.

June 1, 1984
Memphis, Tennessee

THE PRE-MISSION STORY

During the last two decades of the nineteenth century Episcopalians in the community of Germantown, Tennessee from time to time asserted a corporate identity by congregating for services.[1] For the most part, however, those who did attend church regularly were required to travel into Memphis or Collierville each Sunday. In those days a ten-mile trip was not made by motorcar but, at best, by horse and buggy over poor roads. It is little wonder that those of Anglican persuasion in the community attended local churches or none at all.

The Baptists, Methodists, and Presbyterians were fairly well established in Germantown by the latter part of the nineteenth century, although the Baptists and Methodists suffered during the Federal occupation in the Civil War.[2] All three of the denominations during the last half of the century had practiced a spirit of

---

[1] See notes 5, 16, infra.

[2] Paul R. Coppock, "Mid-South Memoirs," The Commercial Appeal, November 9, 1975; Mrs. Clarence A. Smith, History of Germantown Baptist Church (Dallas, Texas: Taylor Publishing Company, 1982), p. 9.

cooperation and sharing.[3] This spirit became helpful to the few fledgling Episcopalians when they began to come together for services.[4] There is no way for us to know when those early Episcopalians first gathered together in homes, but as early as 1885 the Right Reverend Charles T. Quintard, Bishop, held a service in the "chapel" at Bailey's Station east of Germantown.[5] This gathering took place before the organization of St. Andrew's Mission, where many Germantown Episcopalians were communicants.[6] There continued a close relationship between St. Andrew's and Germantown Episcopalians

---

[3] Ibid., p. 7.

[4] Episcopalians were permitted use of the Methodist Church in 1894 and the Presbyterian Church in 1907. See notes 16, 22, infra.

[5] Journal, Diocese of Tennessee, 1885, p. 23. The chapel which the bishop mentions in his diary was a simple frame building located at the northwest corner of Houston-Levee Road and Highway 72. It was maintained for the community by the Bedford and Bailey families. The building was later converted into a residence and through the years it disintegrated and was finally torn down. Interviews with Elizabeth Baker Parr from her recollections of Helen Mangrum Bedford, September, 1983.

[6] St. Andrew's Mission, Collierville, was organized in 1888, Journal, Diocese of Tennessee, 1888.

until 1944, when St. George's achieved parish status.[7]

The first family to produce a descendant directly responsible in part for the establishment of a mission in Germantown was the Yancey family.[8] The Yancey family had been long identified with the Episcopal Church in West Tennessee[9] when Dr. Edwin Yancey settled in Germantown about 1880.[10] Two years earlier he had married Laura Stillwell of Arkansas Post,

---

[7] Both congregations were served by the same clergy from 1934 to 1944.

[8] Among the early Germantown families, the Yanceys were the most active in the Episcopal Church. Other early families whose members also were Episcopalians were the Messicks, Hanks, and Bennetts. Interviews by correspondence with Lotta Lee Adair, 1983.

[9] Dr. Yancey's father was also a physician of the same name in LaGrange, Tennessee, where he was born on December 12, 1852. He attended the College of Physicians and Surgeons in Baltimore, Maryland, before beginning practice in Arkansas Post, Arkansas. Interviews, Lotta Lee Adair, supra; The Memphis Press-Scimitar, June 6, 1933, p. 12. Also see note 13, infra.

[10] The Memphis Press-Scimitar, June 6, 1933, p. 12.

Arkansas,[11] where he had begun his medical practice.[12] With his family background as an initiative, Dr. Yancey became an active churchman in the last decade of the nineteenth century with the intent of Episcopal worship in Germantown.[13] Correspondence to him from then Assistant Bishop Frank Gailor clearly indicates a response to an inquiry by Dr. Yancey to have a service in Germantown.[14] Bishop Gailor's letter in

---

[11] Ibid.

[12] The Memphis Press-Scimitar, June 6, 1933, p. 12.

[13] Dr. Yancey, Senior (Dr. Yancey,II), was the second of three to bear the full name. Through his mother, Mary May Anderson, he is descended from Mary Hayes Willis Closter, the primary founder of Emmanuel Church in LaGrange, Tennessee. Ellen Davies Rogers, The Romance of the Episcopal Church in West Tennessee (Brunswick, Tennessee: Plantation Press, 1964), p. 84.

[14] Bishop Thomas F. Gailor to Dr. E.T. Yancey, October 5, 1893, original given to author by Mrs. Hiram Adair, Gulfstream, Florida, now in the Diocesan Archives, St. Mary's Cathedral, Memphis, Tennessee. See Appendix for text.

1893[15] was followed in 1894 by probably the first public Episcopal service in Germantown and certainly the first by a bishop of the Diocese of Tennessee.[16] The service, which took place in the Methodist Church[17] on a Saturday, was some evidence of the numerical strength of Episcopalians in the community at that time. The bishop commented that several were present for the service, one of whom was the Baptist

---

[15] The service suggested by the bishop's letter apparently did not take place because ten days later he suffered a serious illness. Thomas Frank Gailor, Some Memories, 1908-1935 (Kingsport, Tennessee: Southern Publishers, Inc., 1937), p. 156. In addition the bishop's diary indicates that he was at Sewanee on December 3, 1893, and on December 10, 1893, with no indication he left during the week. Journal, Diocese of Tennessee, 1894, p. 33.

[16] Journal, Diocese of Tennessee, 1894, p. 35.

[17] In 1894 the Methodist Church in Germantown was located near the northwest corner of McVay Road, where it changes direction from south to west. The church was destroyed by fire in the early 1920s, leaving only the old cemetary to the north behind it. Betsy West, "A Short History of the Germantown Methodist Church" (1982).

preacher.[18] Even the most optimistic soul did not need a voice from Heaven announcing that any idea of an Episcopal mission in Germantown at that time was somewhat premature.

After the turn of the century, apparently, services were held periodically in homes.[19] Dr. Yancey's daughter, Lotta Adair, relates that during this period the Reverend Mr. Prentice Pugh at Holy Trinity Church would make visits on the second and fourth Sundays each month to hold afternoon services for Episcopalians in the Germantown Presbyterian Church.[20] The Reverend Mr. Pugh would then return to Memphis, as he had come, by the local train which operated between Memphis and Collierville. Mrs. Adair's recollection of these services appears to be substantially

---

[18] The service took place on Saturday, February 3, 1894. Thomas Frank Gailor, Some Memories, p. 35.

[19] Both Mrs. Adair and Mrs. Louise Acklen suggest that services took place in Yancey and Messick homes. See notes 25, 42, infra.

[20] Lotta Lee Yancey Adair (Mrs. Hiram). Interviews by correspondence with Mrs. Adair and Kathryn Zook, 1983. Also see Founders, infra.

corroborated by Mr. Arthur B. Chambers, a life-long member of Holy Trinity Episcopal Church.[21] While Mrs. Adair and Mr. Chambers differ with respect to the details of the visitations to Germantown by Mr. Pugh, the fact that they did occur is further substantiated by the records of the Germantown Presbyterian Church[22] and Mr. Pugh's own recollections.[23] These visits

---

[21] Mrs. Adair's recollection of Mr. Pugh's visitations to Germantown is corroborated by Mr. A. B. Chambers of Memphis. Mr. Chambers, who was ninety-one years old at this writing, remembers that the visits occurred only once a month and that they were made by motor car rather than by the train. Interview with A. B. Chambers, October, 1983.

[22] The Session records of the Germantown Presbyterian Church are consistent with the recollections of Mrs. Adair and Mr. Chambers. An entry dated April 23, 1907, briefly states the following:
> On motion the Episcopalians were invited to hold their services in the Presbyterian Church at such times as do not conflict with our appointments.

Germantown Presbyterian Church, Session Book 1, p. 49.

[23] The Reverend Mr. Pugh indicated that he received ten dollars a month from Collierville and ten dollars from Germantown, an amount which he recollects was "not bad in those days." Prentice Pugh, Parson Pugh's Memoirs (Nashville, Tennessee: Ambrose Printing Company, 1963), p. 16.

must have occurred between 1907 and 1915.[24] Afterwards, there appeared to be no corporate worship by Episcopalians in Germantown for almost twenty years, except perhaps for that which took place in private homes.[25] A significant example of such a private service occurred on June 6, 1933, with the death of Dr. Edwin Yancey.[26] The funeral service was conducted by the Very Reverend Israel H. Noe, Dean of St. Mary's Cathedral,[27] at the home of Dr. Yancey in Germantown.[28] It was a service well attended by

---

[24] The Reverend Mr. Pugh became Priest-in-Charge of Holy Trinity in 1905, leaving in 1915 to become Rector of the Church of Advent, Nashville, Tennessee. Holy Trinity Episcopal Church, Parish Register, p. 31. Two baptisms are recorded during this period in Germantown: Edwin Shelby Williamson on July 11, 1909, and Laura Lee Williamson on March 12, 1911, both occurring on the second Sunday of the month, pp. 68-69.
[25] Interviews by correspondence, Lotta Lee Yancey Adair, 1983.
[26] The Memphis Press-Scimitar, June 6, 1933, p. 12.
[27] Ibid.
[28] Ibid.

those in the Germantown community, which Dr. Yancey had served as a physician for fifty years.[29] Ironically, it was one year almost to the day after Dr. Yancey's death[30] that his fellow Episcopalians in the community brought into being the first Episcopal church in Germantown, Tennessee.

Ten years prior to his death, Dr. Yancey served on a committee with W. Poston Maury and S. J. Shepherd that was appointed by the bishop to investigate a proposal to exchange a lot on Germantown Road in Germantown for one deeded to the Convention by the Executors of W. W. Bott.[31] Mr. Bott of DeSoto County, Mississippi, who died on March 16, 1903, left a lot in Germantown, Tennessee, as a "church lot" to the

---

[29] Ibid.

[30] The organizational meeting was held in late May or early June in 1934. Louise F. Acklen, "Scrapbook of St. George's Episcopal Church" (1965), Appendix.

[31] Diocesan Records, Resolution of the 91st Annual Convention of the Protestant Episcopal Church in the Diocese of Tennessee, January, 1923. The lot was of low elevation and apparently adjacent to the Southern Railroad right-of-way. Register's Office, Shelby County, Tennessee, Book 364, p. 454.

Episcopal Church.[32] The appointment came as a result of a report to the 1923 Diocesan Convention by the Chancellor, S. J. Shepherd, that the Strickland family of Germantown had offered to exchange a smaller lot on Germantown Road for the lot deeded to the Convention.[33] The committee reported to Bishop Maxon the following January in favor of the proposed exchange with find-

---

[32] Probate Court Records, Shelby County, Tennessee, Will Book 17, p. 274. Mr. Bott's will contained the following provision:
> My lot in Germantown, part of it, one acre, I give for church lot to the Episcopal Church and in fond remembrance of the Rev. John Blount, deceased, of the Lillieshall Parish Church, Salpp, England.

Ibid., pp. 266-267.

[33] Diocesan Records, Report of Chancellor to the 91st Annual Convention, January, 1923. See Document 2, Appendix.

ings that would support no other recommendations.[34] The transaction was consummated when the Convention received title to the Strickland lot on the northeast corner of Germantown Road and Spring Street.[35] The lot was located directly north across Spring Street from the Germantown Masonic Lodge. The stage was now set for the location of the first Episcopal church in Germantown, Tennessee.

There has been some suggestion that an Episcopal church may have existed prior to the turn of the century in the Germantown community.[36] The suggestion

---

[34] Diocesan Records, Report of Chancellor to Convention, January 15, 1924. The report of the Committee advised in favor of the exchange, provided that the Strickland heirs could offer the Convention good title. The basis of the decision was that they found it impossible to identify the property, it was deemed advisable to exchange such title as the Convention may have for the lot offered by the Strickland heirs. See Document 3, Appendix.

[35] Register's Office, Shelby County, Tennessee, Book 992, p. 63.

[36] Louise F. Acklen, "Scrapbook of: The History of St. George's Episcopal Church" (1965). See Document 14, Appendix.

results from the response of Mrs. Acklen[37] to the account given regarding the naming of St. George's Church in The Romance of the Episcopal Church in West Tennessee by Ellen Davies-Rogers.[38] Mrs. Rogers' book indicates that the church was named in memory of George Hanks and George Bennett, who died as small children, their parents being among the founders.[39] Mrs. Acklen correctly points out that the parents of these children were not founders of St. George's Church, but she then goes on to suggest the existence of an Episcopal church in the Germantown community in the 1800s which could have been named for the children.[40] The location of this first Episcopal church is said to have been at the corner of Old Poplar Pike and

---

[37] Ibid.

[38] Ellen Davies-Rogers, The Romance of the Episcopal Church in West Tennessee (Brunswick, Tennessee: Plantation Press, 1964).

[39] Ibid., p. 187.

[40] Acklen, "Scrapbook" history, Appendix.

Kirby Road.[41] The southeast corner was the site of the old Messick family home, where some of the early services in homes could have been held.[42] The historical confusion most probably occurred from the fact that a church house was constructed on the southwest corner of Old Poplar and Kirby Road.[43] A lot in excess of an acre was given specifically for a church lot by Joseph Brooks in August, 1872, to the Cumberland Presbyterian Church.[44] Shortly thereafter the Brookhaven Cumberland Presbyterian Church did come into existence with the construction of the church

---

[41] Ibid.

[42] Interviews by correspondence with Mrs. Lotta Adair, January 25, 1983, and March 1, 1983; interview with Dorothy Kirby Wills, September, 1983.

[43] Deed Records, Office of the Register, Shelby County, Tennessee, Book 86, p. 595.

[44] Id. The deed dated August 9, 1872, required a church house to be built within two years and it be designated as the "Brookhaven Cumberland Presbyterian Church," p. 596.

building, but the church lasted fewer than ten years.[45] After it ceased to be used for a church, the lot reverted back to the Grantor under the terms of the deed.[46] The building was subsequently demolished about 1891 and the lumber used to build the parsonage of the Germantown Baptist Church.[47]

It is quite easy to see how the confusion arose concerning an early Episcopal church in the Germantown community. If an Episcopal church did exist in the Germantown community prior to the organization of St. George's in 1934, there would have been some reference to it in the Diocesan Records or Journals, and such is

---

[45] Cumberland Presbyterian Church, Minutes of Memphis Presbytery, August 23, 24, 26, 1872, p. 8; interview with Jane K. Williamson, Director and Archivist, Historical Foundation of the Cumberland Presbyterian Church, September 28, 1983.

[46] Deed Records, Office of the Register, Shelby County, Tennessee, Book 86, pp. 595-6.

[47] Interviews with Dorothy Kirby Wills, October, 1983. Germantown Baptist Church, Minutes, January 25, 1891.

not the case.[48]

One of the only two living founders, Mrs. Hiram Adair,[49] seems very emphatic that the name "St. George's" was chosen about the beginning of this century.[50] Her recollection is that the choice was made sometime after Bishop Gailor responded to her father's letter in 1893.[51] According to Mrs. Adair, the name of their future church was decided upon by members of

---

[48] The author, with the most able assistance of Canon George Fox, the Diocesan Historiographer, found no reference to an Episcopal mission or church in the Germantown community prior to the organization of St. George's in 1934. Mrs. Acklen, now Rosengarten, still a valued, longtime communicant of St. George's, agrees with the author. Sometime after she had finished the history in the "Scrapbook," she learned that the early church at Poplar Pike and Kirby Road was some other denomination than Episcopal. Interview with Louise Acklen Rosengarten, October 6, 1983.

[49] At this writing, besides Mrs. Adair, only Carl Graves was still living.

[50] Interviews by correspondence with Lotta Adair, January 25, 1983; February 14, 1983; October 7, 1983; and October 31, 1983.

[51] Ibid. See note 14, supra.

the Yancey,[52] Bennett,[53] Messick,[54] and Hanks[55] families in memory of the young, deceased sons of the Bennett and Hanks families, both of whom were named "George."[56] Her account is corroborated again by Mr. Arthur B. Chambers,[57] who recalls that when the

---

[52] See notes 8, 9, 19, supra.

[53] The George Bennett family included the father, mother, and a daughter, Gertrude. They lived in the old Hunter Lane Home at 6256 Poplar. No member of the Bennett family appears to have been connected with the founding of St. George's Mission. Interview by correspondence, Lotta Adair, October 7, 1983.

[54] Members of the Messick family were early Episcopalians in the Germantown community. See notes 8, 42, supra.

[55] Captain and Mrs. Hanks as well as their daughter, Alma (Alymer), later Mrs. Ben Bruce, were all Episcopalians. Interview by correspondence with Lotta Adair, October 7, 1983.

[56] Mrs. Adair is the source of the statement made regarding the name of the mission in Mrs. Rogers' book. Interview with Ellen Davies-Rogers, 1983. Also see notes 38, 39, supra.

[57] See note 21, supra.

Reverend Mr. Pugh made his monthly visits to the Germantown Presbyterian Church,[58] reference was made at that time to his going out to St. George's and not just Germantown.[59] This information indicates that those early Episcopalians had, in fact, come to consider themselves a congregation by the time Mr. Pugh had begun his monthly visits to Germantown, probably sometime in 1907.[60] As further support of Mrs. Adair's recollection, a young son of the Bennetts did die in 1892, and a son of the Hanks died in 1887.[61]

Notwithstanding the strong evidence presented by Mrs. Adair's account, it is still difficult to understand how the Hanks and Bennett families, who were remote to the founding of St. George's Mission, could

---

[58] See notes 22, 23, 24, supra.
[59] Interview with A. B. Chambers, supra.
[60] See notes 22, 24, supra.
[61] George C. Bennett, Jr., age four years, five months, died of scarlet fever on January 24, 1892. George Hanks, age not given, died August 20, 1887, residence, Germantown, Tennessee. Memphis and Shelby County Health Department, Memphis, Tennessee, Vital Records.

have significantly influenced such an important decision.[62] Mrs. Acklen has been more disposed to believe that the mission's name resulted from a corporate decision of the founders based upon several considerations, not the least of which was that many were Anglophiles.[63] Further, even though the founders knew and, no doubt, greatly respected Dr. Edwin Yancey, for the most part they arrived fewer than twenty years prior to the founding of the mission and therefore did not have the benefit of participating in the services at the Germantown Presbyterian Church,

---

[62] No member of the Bennett or Hanks families took part in the organization or support of the mission. Alma Hanks Bruce, whose brother is said to have died young, did become a communicant of St. George's Mission eight years after its founding. Interview by correspondence with Lotta Adair, October 7, 1983; St. George's Episcopal Church, Register 1, p. 50.

[63] Interview with Louise Acklen, now Rosengarten, October 6, 1983. St. George is the patron saint of England.

where they might have been part of that original congregation described by Mrs. Adair.[64]

It is of little matter which theory the reader accepts as historical fact, since it now appears that the church was meant to be named "St. George's." And so it was--St. George's, after the patron saint of England, the complement to its sister to the east in Collierville, St. Andrew's, named for the patron saint of Scotland.

---

[64] Except for Lotta Adair, Mamie Cloyes was the first of the founders to move to Germantown in 1918, well after the monthly services had ended. Interview with Harry Cloyes, February 22, 1983.

THE FOUNDERS   21

　　The twelve persons who were applicants to the bishop for the organization of St. George's Mission in 1934 cannot all be considered founders.[1] Four of those who applied were not founders since their participation was perfunctory or they left the mission shortly after it was organized.[2] There are also two others who most certainly should be considered as founders[3] but who for some reason did not appear on the application. Of those who were founders there were three married couples,[4] one widower,[5] a

---

[1] The application to the bishop appears as Document 4 in the Appendix.

[2] Edwin S. Williamson, Frances Martin, Charles E. Speer, and Elizabeth D. Speer.

[3] Hiram T. Adair and Dorothy G. Walker Kirby.

[4] Carl R. and Mary Hebron Graves, Hiram T. and Lotta Adair, J. A. and Geraldine A. Martin.

[5] John Bell Hebron.

divorcee,[6] and two whose spouses were not Episcopalians.[7] They were an unusual collection of personalities who covered the economic, social, and cultural spectrum, but from every indication there was a corporate, cooperative spirit that permeated the group, which was a necessity for success in those years of economic depression.[8]

It is indeed fortunate for the author that those who are named herein as founders have already been so designated by two of our past chroniclers who were

---

[6] Mamie Cloyes.

[7] John B. Scruggs and Dorothy G. Walker Kirby. Mrs. Scruggs (Pearl) was later confirmed on November 14, 1937. St. George's Episcopal Church, Register No. 1, p. 98; Joseph Kirby remained a Baptist even though he was supportive of the new mission financially and through the work of his wife. Interviews with Dorothy Kirby Wills, 1982, 1983.

[8] Interviews with Harry F. Cloyes and Robert C. Lanier, 1982, 1983.

better advised to make such a determination.[9] In retrospect it appears to the author that their judgment was correct. Of the four who signed the application to the bishop not designated as founders, two took no discernible part in the organization or activities of the mission.[10] While the other two did take part in the initial organization, they remained little more than a year thereafter, not being present during the first crucial and formative years of the mission.[11]

The short biographical sketches which follow include not only those of the founders, but also those four not considered founders who joined in the application to the bishop. From a historical standpoint it is felt that the latter should be included

---

[9] Pearl Scruggs, "History of the Mission in Germantown, Tennessee," Unpublished, Document 8, Appendix; Louise F. Acklen, "Scrapbook of St. George's Episcopal Church" (1965), Unpublished. Document 14, Appendix.

[10] Edwin S. Williamson and Frances Martin.

[11] Charles E. Speer and Elizabeth D. Speer.

since they did take part in the initial organization.

There is always great risk in assigning more importance to one or several who undertook such a corporate effort. The order in which the biographies appear is based upon the function and office the individual served in the organization and initial operation of the new mission.

JOHN BRIDGES SCRUGGS - 1886 - 1955

JOHN BRIDGES SCRUGGS

In 1934 John B. Scruggs and his wife, Pearl O'Neil Scruggs, lived at 2220 Germantown Road, Germantown Road, Germantown, Tennessee.[12] At that time he was a communicant of St. Andrew's in Collierville, where he had recently become a layreader.[13] While there appeared to be a universal desire among Germantown Episcopalians for a church in Germantown, it was John Scruggs who gave impetus to the movement.[14] Without question, he enlisted the aid and advice of the Venerable Charles K. Weller, Archdeacon, in the establishment of the mission at Germantown. Scruggs as well as others had been commuting to Collierville or to Memphis each Sunday.[15] Even though there were relatively few Episcopalians in Germantown, John Scruggs was not dissuaded by that fact.[16] After the

---

[12] Interview with Ednamae Thompson, April, 1983.
[13] Scruggs, "History," supra. He became a layreader as early as January, 1932. John Scruggs, "Scrapbook."
[14] Interview with Kenneth Robertson, April, 1983.
[15] Ibid.
[16] Scruggs, "History," supra.

organizational meeting in early June 1934, he was primarily responsible for securing the use of the lower floor of the Germantown Masonic Lodge for services.[17] This location made possible weekly services for Germantown Episcopalians, giving them identity as a church.

During the period from 1934 to 1940 John Scruggs was, in effect, the clergy of St. George's Mission since the Diocese supplied a priest only once a month for Eucharist.[18] Even after 1940 when there was a priest in residence,[19] Scruggs continued to serve as layreader.[20]

---

[17] Germantown F & AM Lodge, Minutes, July 26, 1934. These Minutes indicate "Bro. J. B. Scruggs paid on the light bill for the use of the ground floor for Episcopal Services." Scruggs was not a member of the Lodge at the time, but he was a member of Lodge No. 266 in Greenville, Mississippi. Subsequently, he apparently thought it prudent to become affiliated and made the appropriate application, which was approved. Minutes, January 17, 1936; February 20, 1936.

[18] Interview with Kenneth Robertson, April 26, 1983.

[19] Living Church Annual (Yearbook of the Episcopal Church), 1941, pp. 318-319.

[20] Interview with Kenneth Robertson, supra.

While the Vestry Minutes reflect that Mr. Scruggs was elected senior warden in 1949, the Diocesan Parochial Report for that year reported Turk Humphrey as senior warden. From those records the mission reported that Mr. Scruggs served as treasurer from 1935 through 1937 and vestry clerk from 1940 through 1943.[21] He became less active in the three years before his death in 1955 because of illness.[22]

Mr. Scruggs was born August 11, 1886, in Arkansas City, Arkansas, but was reared in Greenville, Mississippi.[23] After service in World War I, he moved to

---

[21] Vestry Minutes, St. George's Episcopal Church, February 14, 1949. Records, Diocese of Tennessee, Parochial Reports of St. George's Mission and Church.

[22] Scruggs suffered from Parkinson's disease. Interview with Kenneth Robertson; Register No. 2, St. George's Episcopal Church, p. 146.

[23] Interview with Isabelle Scruggs Wade, May 22, 1983. The son of John Bridges Scruggs and Virginia Wilbourn Scruggs, John Scruggs later attended the University of the South at Sewanee and Centre College in Danville, Kentucky. The Memphis Commercial Appeal, September 5, 1955, p. 22,

Memphis in 1925.[24] He came to Germantown as a result of his marriage to Pearl O'Neil, in whose home they began married life.[25]

Shortly after he came to Memphis, Mr. Scruggs was employed by the Memphis District of the U. S. Corps of Engineers, a position he held for twenty-three years until retirement.[26] His death in 1955 followed three years after his retirement.[27]

John Scruggs' wife, Pearl, was born Nellie Pearl O'Neil in 1893. Her father, Arthur O'Neil, immigrated from Ireland in 1853 and eventually settled in Germantown.[28] Her mother was Nellie Conn O'Neil, the niece

---

[24] Ibid.

[25] Interview with Isabelle Scruggs Wade, supra.

[26] The Memphis Commercial Appeal, September 5, 1955, p. 22.

[27] John Scruggs died September 4, 1955, with burial in Memorial Park, Memphis, on September 5, 1955. Register No. 2, pp. 146-147.

[28] Mrs. Clarence A. Smith, History of Germantown Baptist Church (Dallas, Texas: Taylor Publishing Company, 1982), p. 24.

of William Twyford,[29] with whom she lived after being orphaned at the age of two.[30] Even though she was christened in the Catholic Church,[31] Pearl grew up attending the Baptist Church because of its proximity.

The enthusiasm and dedication of John Scruggs in the establishment of an Episcopal mission in Germantown obviously affected his wife. We are greatly indebted to her chronicles on the early history of the mission.[32] In them there is an understandable empha-

---

[29] William Twyford is said to have been Germantown's first settler. Id.

[30] Twyford is reported in 1854 to have become her guardian; however, Shelby County Probate records disclose no appointment of a legal guardian in that year. He probably only undertook the care and support of his niece. Id.

[31] She was christened December 19, 1893, in St. Mary's Catholic Church, Register, 1860-96.

[32] Her history amounted to several typewritten pages which are discussed in the section devoted to sources. See Documents 6, 8, Appendix. Mrs. Scruggs was a teacher at Mabel C. Williams High School, now Germantown High School. Interviews, Kenneth Robertson, supra.

sis on the part played by her husband in the founding of the mission.[33] Her devotion and respect for him are easily understood by the fact that no sooner had the mission come into existence than she became an Episcopalian.[34] After the death of her husband, she returned to the Germantown Baptist Church.[35] At this writing Mrs. Scruggs was still living though confined to a nursing home.[36]

---

[33] Mrs. Scruggs' position was supported by Archdeacon Weller, probably the best authority to make such a judgment. Archdeacon Weller said of Mr. Scruggs, "I feel that without the influence of John B. Scruggs there will not be any St. George's Church there." (Germantown) Archdeacon Weller to Pearl Scruggs, April 10, 1944. See Document 11, Appendix.

[34] She was confirmed at St. George's Mission on November 11, 1937, by Bishop Maxon. St. George's, Register No. 1, pp. 98-99.

[35] St. George's, Register No. 2, p. 55. Smith, History, supra, p. 24.

[36] Hillhaven Convalescent Center, Memphis, Tennessee.

JOHN BELL HEBRON 1860 - 1942

HEBRON WINDOW

JOHN BELL HEBRON

John Hebron was seventy-four years old when he became the first warden of St. George's Mission, Germantown, Tennessee. He was not then the senior warden because he was appointed by Bishop James M. Maxon as part of the Bishop's Committee for the Mission.[36]

John Hebron was born in 1860 in Warren County (Vicksburg), Mississippi, the son of Col. John L. Hebron and Adine Hebron.[37] During the Civil War the Hebrons' plantation home became headquarters for several Federal generals, one of whom was U. S. Grant. The story was told that each morning as General Grant descended the stairs from his quarters, he picked up young John; while being held, the child permissively pulled the general's whiskers.[38]

---

[36] Louise Finley Acklen, "Scrapbook of the History of St. George's Episcopal Church," Unpublished, 1965. See Document 14, Appendix.

[37] The Memphis Press-Scimitar, November 6, 1942, p. 21.

[38] The story was told Mr. Hebron by his mother and repeated by him during his long life. Ibid., p. 21.

Prior to joining Armour and Company in 1903, John Hebron operated a plantation in Washington County (Greenville), Mississippi, and in 1896 became the sheriff of that county.[39] It was in Greenville that the paths of two of the future partners in faith of St. George's Mission could have crossed but for the age differential. John Scruggs was about ten years old when Mr. Hebron became sheriff at thirty-six.[40] However, Scruggs was surely in his mid-teens before Hebron left Greenville, which had only one Episcopal parish at that time.[41]

In 1930 John Hebron retired as the Southern

---

[39] Ibid. He married Nannie Laura Burdette June 23, 1897; both were confirmed the next day. St. James' Episcopal Church, Greenville, Mississippi, Parish Register. Difference in the spelling of names is not unusual in church records.

[40] John Scruggs was born August 11, 1886. Interview and family history with Isabelle Scruggs Wade, May 21, 1983. See note 37.

[41] Hebron was confirmed at St. James, January 24, 1897, and Scruggs, February 5, 1899. St. James Episcopal Church Register.

District Manager of Armour and Company and thereafter moved to Germantown.[42] Before the organization of St. George's the Hebrons were communicants of Calvary Church in Memphis.[43] After the death of his wife in 1934, he lived with his daughter and son-in-law at 7400 Crestridge in Germantown.[44] As a memorial to his wife, a stained-glass window depicting the Madonna and Child was given by Mr. Hebron to the new mission.[45] It was placed over the altar in the chapel

---

[42] See note 37.

[43] While there appears to be no record of the Hebrons' membership in the Calvary Parish Register, they are listed as communicants of Calvary Episcopal Church, Inc., in a 1925 compilation by the Reverend Mr. Charles F. Blaisdell. Ellen Davies Rogers, The Great Book, Calvary Protestant Episcopal Church, Memphis, Tennessee, 1832-1972 (Brunswick, Tennessee: Plantation Press, 1973), p. 826.

[44] His daughter, Mary Ellen, married a lawyer, Carl R. Graves, both of whom were among the original ten. The Memphis Press-Scimitar, November 6, 1942; interviews with early mission communicants, 1982, 1983; The Memphis Commercial Appeal, November 6, 1942.

[45] Acklen, "Scrapbook," supra. The inscription on the window is "Nanie Burnett Hebron Born 1870 Died 1934."

when it was completed in March, 1937.[46]

Mr. Hebron was appointed warden initially by the bishop as a member of the Bishop's Committee.[47] Subsequently, he served as senior warden by election until his death on November 6, 1942.[48] The Reverend Mr. Charles L. Widney conducted the service on November 7, 1942, with the burial in Memorial Cemetery.[49]

---

[46] Ibid.

[47] Pearl Scruggs, "History of the Mission in Germantown, Tennessee," Unpublished, 1937-38. Document 8, Appendix.

[48] While there are no extant vestry minutes for that period, the parochial reports of the mission indicate Mr. Hebron as senior warden through the year 1942. Tennessee Diocesan Records.

[49] St. George's Episcopal Church, Register No. 1, p. 110.

Inside Original Chapel

Mr & Mrs. Hiram T. Adair
50th Wedding Anniversary August 10, 1972

HIRAM TYRE ADAIR - LOTTA LEE YANCEY ADAIR

Hiram Tyre Adair was born on November 30, 1897, in Paris, Kentucky. Lotta Lee Yancey was born on February 11, 1896, in Germantown, Tennessee, the daughter of Dr. Edwin Thomas Yancey, II, one of the early Germantown Episcopalians.[50] The couple met and were later married in Calvary Church on August 10, 1922. When the mission began in 1934, they resided at 7475 Old Poplar Pike in Germantown, Tennessee, her parents' home until their deaths in 1933.[51]

Lottie, as she prefers to be called, was one of the original petitioners[52] to establish the mission in which she later served as secretary and treasurer of the Women's Auxiliary.[53] Mr. Adair, while not a

---

[50] Interviews by correspondence with Lotta Adair and Kathryn Zook, 1983. Dr. Yancey was discussed in the pre-mission story, infra.

[51] Both of Mrs. Adair's parents died in 1933, Dr. Yancey on June 6, 1933, and her mother, Laura Stilwell Yancey, on November 9, 1933. Interviews, supra.

[52] Journal, Diocese of Tennessee, 1935, p. 83.

[53] Interviews, supra.

petitioner, was clearly one of the founders. Together with John Hebron, he supervised the construction of the chapel, the first church building.[54] Mr. Adair later served on the vestry and in 1955 was junior warden.[55]

Born to the Adairs were two daughters. Kathryn Stilwell Adair, now Mrs. Morgan M. Zook, was born July 29, 1927. Nancy Yancey Adair, now Mrs. Devereaux Cannon, was born January 16, 1932.

In 1947 the Adairs moved to Ellendale, Tennessee, where their daughter Nancy still resides.[56] Mr. Adair operated the Adair Heating and Plumbing Company for many years prior to his death on April 12, 1980.[57] Mrs. Adair moved to Gulfstream, Florida, in July, 1982, where she resides with her daughter Kathryn and her son-in-law, Morgan Zook.

---

[54] Acklen, "Scrapbook," supra.

[55] Vestry Minutes, St. George's Episcopal Church, January 6, 1955. The Parochial Report for the year 1954 indicates he was also junior warden during that year. Tennessee Diocesan Records, supra.

[56] Interviews, supra.

[57] Commercial Appeal, April 12, 1980, p. C-4.

40

Mr. & Mrs. Carl Richmond Graves

Carl Richmond Graves was born on November 18, 1901, in Memphis, Tennessee, the son of Richmond Lee Graves and Carrie J. Graves.[58] He attended Lauderdale Grade School and Central High in Memphis, and later Cumberland University in Lebanon, Tennessee. He was admitted to the Bar in 1921 and began the practice of law in Memphis.[59]

Mary Ellen Hebron, later nicknamed "Chick," was born on October 22, 1903, in Greenville, Mississippi. She was the daughter of John Bell Hebron, the mission's first warden, and Nanie B. Hebron. Also attending Central High in Memphis, she married Mr. Graves on November 20, 1924.[60] They became members of Calvary Episcopal Church, Memphis, where they had been married, with their confirmation on January 25, 1925.[61] Their membership continued at Calvary until 1934 with

---

[58] Interview with Carl R. Graves, March 15, 1983.
[59] Ibid.
[60] Ibid.
[61] Calvary Episcopal Church, Register, 1925, p. 24.

the founding of the mission. As applicants to the bishop for St. George's Mission, by that action they became members of the new mission.[62]

In 1930 the Graves moved to Germantown, Tennessee.[63] When the mission was organized in 1934, Mr. Graves, first a member of the "Bishop's Committee," became the mission's first junior warden for the year 1935 and continued in that capacity until 1943, when he served as senior warden after the death of John Hebron.[64]

Born to the Graves were two sons, both of whom were confirmed at St. George's Mission:[65] Carl Hebron, who now lives in Michigan, and John Lawrence, who is deceased.

---

[62] Constitution and Canons of the Diocese of Tennessee, 1940, Canon 17.

[63] The Graves lived in a house which is now 7400 Crestridge Road, Germantown.

[64] Diocesan Archives, St. Mary's Cathedral, Memphis, Tennessee, Parochial Reports of St. George's Mission, 1934-1943.

[65] St. George's Episcopal Church, Register 1, pp. 98 and 102.

In 1948 the Graves moved back to Memphis and transferred their membership to Grace-St. Luke's Episcopal Church,[66] where they remained until Mr. Graves' retirement in 1972 after serving many years as a United States Referee in Bankruptcy.[67]

Mrs. Graves died June, 1979, and at this writing Mr. Graves, having remarried, resides in Destin, Florida.[68]

---

[66] Grace-St. Luke's Episcopal Church, Register 2, pp. 313-314.

[67] Interview by correspondence with Jean D. Graves, March 9, 1984.

[68] Ibid.

DOROTHY WALKER KIRBY

Dorothy Gordon Walker was born in Memphis, Tennessee, on June 25, 1896. She was the daughter of Richard Gordon Walker and Olive Blanche Lyes Walker. During her early childhood the family lived at 750 Vance Avenue and attended church only a few blocks away at Grace Episcopal Church at the corner of Lauderdale.[69]

When she was about eleven years old, her childhood was marred by tragedy with the death of her mother. Dorothy was enrolled in St. Mary's Boarding School, from which she later graduated, attending Columbia Institute in Columbia, Tennessee.[70]

Dorothy married Joseph Brooks Kirby on October 12, 1920. The couple moved to what was then the country west of Germantown at 6792 Old Poplar Pike.[71] Prior to the organization of St. George's Mission they

---

[69] Interviews with Dorothy Kirby Wills, September and October, 1983.
[70] Ibid.
[71] The house still stands on the north side of Old Poplar Pike (Park) just east of Kirby Parkway. Id.

attended Grace Church on Easter and Christmas and
Germantown Baptist Church more often because of its
proximity.[72]

Born to the Kirbys were two daughters. Dorothy
Gordon Kirby, now Mrs. Walter D. Wills, was born January 31, 1923. Louise Ann Kirby, now Mrs. W. James
Ellis, was born December 23, 1929, and now resides in
Knoxville, Tennessee. Mrs. Wills is a longtime member of St. George's and resides at 2005 Kirbywills
Cove in Memphis.[73]

Dorothy Kirby, like Hiram Adair, for some reason
was not present to sign the application to the bishop;
however, she certainly met all the requisites to classify her as founder.[74] She took part in the organizational acitivities of the mission, but probably her
primary contribution came in the financing of the construction of the first church building, the chapel.
Considering the economic conditions of the mid-nine-

---

[72] Ibid.
[73] Ibid.
[74] See notes 10, 11, supra.

teen-thirties, the Kirbys were relatively comfortable from Mr. Kirby's farming business.[75] No doubt because of his wife, Joseph Kirby, a Baptist,[76] also became a strong supporter of the new mission both financially and through the work of his wife. The Kirbys not only supported fund-raising projects for the construction of the chapel, but Joseph Kirby also pledged funds for that purpose to be matched by contributions from members of the congregation.[77]

After the completion of the chapel, Dorothy Kirby continued to be active in the mission, serving as the first United Thank Offering custodian and later as president of the Women's Auxiliary.[78] She contin-

---

[75] Interviews with Dorothy K. Wills, supra.

[76] Joseph Kirby's ancestors were identified for several generations with the Baptist Church. His great-grandfather, Wilks Brooks, gave the land on which the Germantown Baptist Church was built. Id. Mrs. Clarence A. Smith, History of Germantown Baptist Church (Dallas, Texas: Taylor Publishing Company, 1982), p. 6.

[77] Interviews with Dorothy K. Wills, supra. Also see Acklen, "Scrapbook History," Appendix.

[78] Ibid. Appendix.

ued to be an active member of St. George's until the death of her husband in 1950, when she moved back to Memphis.[79] Later she moved to Knoxville, Tennessee, where her younger daughter, Louise Ann, resided. Dorothy Kirby died in her eightieth year on January 11, 1976, in Knoxville.[80] Burial was in Elmwood Cemetery, Memphis, Tennessee.

---

[79] She transferred to the Church of the Holy Communion in 1952. St. George's Episcopal Church, Register No. 1, p. 43.

[80] St. George's Episcopal Church, Register No. 4, pp. 190-191.

JOSEPH A. MARTIN - GERALDINE A. MARTIN
FRANCES W. MARTIN

Joseph Abram Martin was born on September 30, 1881, in Little Rock, Arkansas. His grandfather, William E. Woodruff, founder of the Arkansas Gazette, influenced young Joe to seek his fortune in the newspaper business.[81] He came to Memphis at the age of sixteen, serving as secretary to the publisher of the Evening Scimitar, the forerunner of the Press-Scimitar. After a stint with the Progressive Farmer and a Birmingham publication, he returned to Memphis, entering the insurance business, first with the Travelers Insurance Company and finally with New York Life.[82]

Geraldine Apperson Martin was born at Scanlin Landing, Arkansas, on October 27, 1891, the daughter of Edmund Minetry Apperson, II, of Memphis and Evans

---

[81] Interviews with John Apperson, Sr., Virginia Falls Apperson, May Apperson Keyes, Dale Apperson Kerr, and Leroy Kerr by Barbara Apperson, 1983. John Apperson is the brother of Geraldine Martin; Virginia is his wife; and May Keyes is his daughter.

[82] Ibid.

Dale Jefferies of Holly Springs, Mississippi.[83]

The Martins were married on April 10, 1918, in Grace Church in Memphis.[84] Born to them were a daughter, Frances Woodruff Martin, and a son, Joseph Junior, who died in infancy. After moving from Memphis to the healthier environs of Forest Hill, Tennessee, where both Mrs. Martin's grandparents had lived, the Martins made their home at what is now 3203 Forest Hill Road, which they named "Martindale."[85]

The beginning of the great adventure for the founders took place in the livingroom of "Martindale" in 1934. It was in the Martins' home that the founding congregation with the aid and advice of Archdeacon Charles Weller became in spirit St. George's Mission.[86]

All three of the Martin family were applicants to

---

[83] Ibid.

[84] Grace Episcopal Church, Register, 1918, p. 400.

[85] Interviews, supra.

[86] Louise F. Acklen, "Scrapbook of St. George's Episcopal Church" (1965), Unpublished. Appendix.

the bishop; however, Frances has not been considered a founder as have her parents, since she took little or no part in the mission's activities other than signing the application.[87] Her parents took part in the fund-raising activities and other efforts to establish the mission. Mr. Martin, appointed to the "Bishop's Committee," became the first secretary of the vestry,[88] and Mrs. Martin was the first president of the Women's Auxiliary.[89]

Several years after the mission was organized, the Martins moved back to Memphis because of Mr. Martin's failing health. He died shortly thereafter on December 28, 1939.[90]

---

[87] See note 10, supra.

[88] Acklen, "Scrapbook," supra.

[89] Pearl Scruggs, "New Episcopal Mission at Germantown Now Completed," (1937), Unpublished. Appendix.

[90] Interviews, supra.

Mrs. Martin transferred her membership to Grace-St. Luke's, where she faithfully and conscientiously served on the altar guild until poor health forced her to move to the Ave Maria Home.[91] She died on September 17, 1974, only to be followed several years later by her daughter, then Frances M. Butterworth, in Charlotte, North Carolina.[92]

---

[91] During the thirty-five years Mrs. Martin was widowed, she became affectionately known as "Aunt Pinky" to her nieces and nephews. Ibid.

[92] Ibid. The author is indebted to Mrs. Barbara Apperson for the research and composition of the preceding biographical sketches.

MRS. HARRY ("MAMIE") CLOYES

MARIE (MAMIE) THERESIA CLOYES

Mamie Cloyes was born Marie Theresia von Arx on November 18, 1893, in St. Louis, Missouri, of Swiss immigrants.[93] While she was still a baby, her parents returned to Switzerland and lived in Olten.[94]

When she was about seventeen, she returned to the United States with her aunt and uncle and lived with them in Memphis, Tennessee.[95] In Memphis she met Harry Cloyes of Union City, Tennessee, and they were married in 1917. They moved to Germantown, Tennessee, in 1918, where Mamie started a flower business in 1920. The Cloyes' only child, a son, Harry, was born in 1926. Three years later there was a separation which ended in divorce.[96]

---

[93] Interview with Harry F. Cloyes, February 22, 1983.
[94] Mamie attended school in both Switzerland and France. Ibid.
[95] She returned in 1910 with her aunt and uncle, Maria and Fritz Hussy, who operated a grocery store at 424 South Lauderdale in Memphis. Ibid.
[96] Ibid.

Prior to her involvement in St. George's Mission,[97] she had not been a regular communicant of any church. She became enthusiastic about the organization of the new mission as a result of her social and civic friendships with the other women who joined in the formation of the new mission.[98] The flower shop which she operated in her home naturally led to an interest in the office which came to be her niche in the mission.[99] She became "Directress of the Altar Guild,"[100] and in that capacity she gave the mission its first altar cloth.[101] In addition, for more than

---

[97] While there is no documentary evidence, Mamie was probably reared a Roman Catholic. Interview with Harry Cloyes, May 9, 1983. It appears, though, that she was baptised and confirmed in that church. Register, No. 1, St. George's Episcopal Church, p. 162.
[98] Interview with Harry F. Cloyes, supra.
[99] Mamie lived at 7831 Old Poplar Pike, Germantown, Tennessee. Ibid.
[100] St. George's "Herald," September, 1941.
[101] Scruggs, "History," supra. Appendix.

twenty years she donated flowers for the altar.[102]

Mamie Cloyes on January 16, 1978, at the age of eighty-four.[103]

CHARLES E. SPEER AND ELIZABETH SPEER

Charles Everett Speer and Elizabeth Dodge were married on April 17, 1918, in Chicago, Illinois. They lived in Memphis until about 1927, when they moved to Germantown, Tennessee, Mr. Speer's birthplace. They continued to be members and communicants of Calvary Church in Memphis until St. George's Mission began in 1934.[104] Prior to his marriage to Elizabeth, Mr. Speer had served on the vestry at Calvary Church.[105]

---

[102] Interviews, supra.

[103] Burial was in Elmwood Cemetery, Memphis, Tennessee. Register No. 5, St. George's Episcopal Church, pp. 258-259.

[104] Interviews with Elizabeth Speer McGehee, 1982, 1983. Mrs. McGehee, the daughter, lives at 191 South Perkins, Memphis, Tennessee, and attends St. John's Episcopal Church.

[105] He served on the vestry in 1905, 1906, 1907, 1915, and 1916, in which year he also served as clerk. Ellen Davies Rogers, The Great Book of Calvary Protestant Episcopal Church, Memphis, Tennessee, 1832-1972 (Brunswick, Tennessee: Planatation Press, 1973), pp. 767-768.

Mr. Speer operated his own real estate business and was active in the social and civic affairs of the community.[106]

At the time the Speers became applicants to the bishop for the establishment of St. George's Mission,[107] they lived in a house that stood at 7351 Old Poplar Pike in Germantown.[108] Mr. Speer was appointed to the Bishop's Committee as the first treasurer of the new mission by Bishop Maxon.[109] The Speers cannot be considered as founders since they remained active only a short time, leaving in 1935.[110] Mrs. Speer and

---

[106] He was a founder of Colonial Country Club and took part in the organization of the Memphis Real Estate Board. The Commercial Appeal, Memphis, Tennessee, July 30, 1961.

[107] Journal, Diocese of Tennessee, 1935, p. 83.

[108] Interviews with Elizabeth Speer McGehee, supra.

[109] Journal, p. 117.

[110] The marriage ended in divorce on December 28, 1935. Shelby County Circuit Court Minute Book 88, p. 202.

their daughter moved back to Memphis, as did Mr. Speer subsequent to the sale of the home.[111] Mr. Speer died in 1961 and Mrs. Speer in 1964.[112]

EDWIN S. WILLIAMSON

Edwin Shelby Williamson was born in Bartlett, Tennessee, on April 4, 1909, the son of John Shelby Williamson and Fannie Mae Yancey.[113] He received his first name from his maternal grandfather, Dr. Edwin T. Yancey, Senior, and his middle name from his father, a direct descendant of Governor Isaac Shelby,[114] for

---

[111] The house subsequently was destroyed by fire, but another has since been built on the lot. Interviews, supra.

[112] Calvary Episcopal Church, Parish Register.

[113] Interviews with Teresa W. Bledsoe, August, September, and October, 1983. Mrs. Bledsoe is a sister of Edwin Williamson and presently a communicant of St. Elizabeth's Episcopal Church.

[114] Ibid. Edwin was baptized on March 12, 1911, in Germantown by the Reverend Mr. Prentice Pugh, probably in the Germantown Presbyterian Church. Register No. 1, Holy Trinity Episcopal Church, pp. 68-69.

whom Shelby County, Tennessee, was named.[115] His adolescent years were spent with grandparents in Germantown, where he graduated from high school.[116] He later joined the William R. Moore Dry Goods Company in Memphis.

In 1934 when Edwin was twenty-five years old, he became one of the applicants to the bishop for the organization of St. George's Mission.[117] Edwin Williamson never became a member of the congregation of of the mission and apparently took no active part in

---

[115] John M. Keating, <u>History of the City of Memphis and Shelby County, Tennessee</u>, Vol. I (Syracuse, New York: D. Mason, 1888), p. 131.

[116] Interviews with Teresa W. Bledsoe, supra. Edwin had the nickname "Puddin" during high school days. Interviews with Kenneth Robertson, 1982, 1983.

[117] Journal, Diocese of Tennessee, 1935, p. 83.

its organization other than signing the application to the bishop.[118] However, he may have attended services of the mission in the Germantown Lodge before his marriage to Ada Strong about 1935.[119]

In the early 1940s Mr. Williamson moved to Chicago, Illinois, where he joined another dry goods firm. He died there on February 28, 1954.[120]

---

[118] Interviews with Teresa W. Bledsoe and Kenneth Robertson, supra. The absence of Williamson's name from the Parish Registers does not preclude his possibly having been a communicant prior to 1940. See The Sources, infra.
[119] Ada Strong, a Baptist who lived at Bailey (Station), and Edwin were childhood sweethearts. Interviews with Teresa W. Bledsoe, supra.
[120] Ibid.

EDWIN SHELBY WILLIAMSON

THE MISSION YEARS

The idea of an Episcopal mission in Germantown had been nurtured by Edwin T. Yancey, Sr., long before John Scruggs and the other founders actually accomplished it.[1] It was a fitting tribute and memorial to Yancey and to that early congregation when their brothers and sisters in Christ organized an Episcopal mission in Germantown. It was to this end that the aid of Archdeacon Charles Weller was enlisted probably by John Scruggs, then a layreader at St. Andrew's in Collierville.[2] Archdeacon Weller is said to have advised Scruggs of a lot owned by the Diocese in Germantown available for the construction of a church building.[3]

John Scruggs then began to give leadership to those with a common desire for an Episcopal mission in

---

[1] Interview by correspondence with Lotta Adair, 1983.
[2] Pearl Scruggs, "New Episcopal Mission at Germantown Now Completed," 1937, Unpublished. See Document 6, Appendix.
[3] Ibid.

Germantown. Notwithstanding that they were few in number, there appeared to be enthusiastic support from the Germantown Episcopalians. A meeting of "all the communicants in the neighborhood"[4] was called at which presumably all the founders were present. Here there seems to be some confusion in the early chronicles with reference to the date.[5] In her history Mrs. Acklen has probably resolved this confusion by placing the organizational meeting at the home of Mr. and

---

[4] Ibid.

[5] In one of Mrs. Scruggs' accounts of the history she indicates that the organizational meeting was held on June 17, 1934. Ibid. Another account indicates that this meeting was held about the first of June, 1934, with the first service held Sunday morning, June 17, at 11:00 A.M. of the same year. Pearl Scruggs, "History of the Mission in Germantown, Tennessee," Unpublished. See Document 8, Appendix.

Mrs. Joseph Martin[6] "about the first of June, 1934" with the "first official service" of the new mission on Sunday morning, June 17, 1934, at eleven o'clock.[7] While the mission had been organized and had had its first service with the blessing of the Archdeacon of West Tennessee,[8] it had no canonical status with the Diocese of Tennessee. This status was not achieved until later in the year when the application to the

---

[6] The Martin home in Forest Hill, Tennessee, where the organizational meeting took place, still stands at 3203 Forest Hill Road, the second house on the west south of the Southern Railroad tracks on Forest Hill Road. Interviews with Robert (Bobby) Lanier and Kenneth Robertson, May, 1983.

[7] Louise Acklen, "Scrapbook of: The History of St. George's Episcopal Church of Germantown, Tennessee," 1965, Unpublished. See Document 14, Appendix.

[8] Charles K. Weller was Archdeacon of West Tennessee from 1930 to 1937, when he retired. Diocesan Archives, St. Mary's Cathedral, Memphis, Tennessee.

bishop was presented to the Diocese.[9] In response to the application Bishop Maxon appointed what was known as the "Bishop's Committee," which was composed of the following individuals:

>John B. Scruggs, Layreader
>J. B. Hebron, Warden
>Joseph A. Martin, Secretary
>Charles Speer, Treasurer
>Carl R. Graves
>Hiram T. Adair

While not technically a vestry, the "committee" did function as such.[10]

---

[9] The application is dated August 1, 1934, as are the applications of other missions presented that year. See Document 4, Appendix. Journal, Diocese of Tennessee, 1935, p. 83.

[10] Acklen, "History," supra. This group was, in effect, the first vestry appointed by the bishop to serve until January 1, 1935. Canon 17 authorized the bishop to make such an appointment. Constitution and Canons of the Diocese of Tennessee, 1940, Canon 17.

GERMANTOWN MASONIC LODGE HALL-CIRCA 1932

What can now be called St. George's second congregation[11] began its services in the Germantown Masonic Lodge Hall.[12] The new mission's first parochial report, which covered the period from September 1, 1934, to January 1, 1935, provided the Diocese with the following information:

> John B. Hebron, Warden
> Joseph Martin, Clerk
> Charles Speer, Treasurer
> John B. Scruggs, Layreader
> Baptized Persons - 31
> Communicants - 17
> Confirmation - 1
> Church Property - $500.00
> Receipts from all sources - $131.43.[13]

Thus, while St. George's began with the first service as a congregation on Sunday, June 17, 1934, its status with the Diocese of Tennessee did not commence until August 1, 1934, the application date to the bishop. Even so, no action was taken on the application until it was presented the following year to the

---

[11] See Note 60, Pre-Mission, supra.
[12] Scruggs, "New Episcopal Mission," supra.
[13] Journal, Diocese of Tennessee, 1935, p. 117.

Diocesan Convention by the bishop coadjutor.[14] The mission was formally admitted to the Diocese on Thursday, January 24, 1935, by the convention.[15]

The first service of the mission is well documented.[16] As has been mentioned, John Scruggs arranged for the use of the Germantown Masonic Lodge Hall,[17] where the first service most probably took place. He negotiated what appeared to be a favorable arrangement to the mission whereby the mission would pay

---

[14] Ibid., p. 22.

[15] Ibid., p. 31.

[16] The date "June 17, 1934" is inscribed on the inside cover of the first mission register in Archdeacon Weller's handwriting. Also see early accounts reprinted in Appendix. This date was misprinted as "June 13, 1934," in the recent book on the new Diocese of West Tennessee. Ellen Davies Rogers, Heirs Through Hope (Brunswick, Tennessee: The Plantation Press, 1983), p. 133. As further support, an article appeared in The Commercial Appeal on Monday, June 18, 1934, reporting the organization of the mission.

[17] Scruggs, "History of the Mission in Germantown, Tennessee," 1937, Unpublished. See Document 8, Appendix.

part of the monthly light (electric) bill in return for the use of the ground floor of the hall.[18] The payment of fifty cents a month represented about one-third of the monthly electric bill.[19] This arrangement continued for a period of almost three years during which the mission used the Lodge Hall. It is interesting to note that during the thirty-three month residency, the mission seems to have missed several payments; however, the Brothers of the Lodge took no punitive action. Finally, in April, 1937, the Lodge received a letter from John B. Hebron, the Senior Warden, thanking the members for the use of Lodge Hall.[20]

---

[18] Minutes, Germantown F & AM Lodge No. 95, July 26, 1934. On this occasion "Bro. J. B. Scruggs paid $1.00" on the light bill. From the method of payment in subsequent months, the one dollar was payment for June and July, 1934.

[19] The monthly amount required of the mission is reflected in subsequent Minutes, supra, June 27, 1935, October 31, 1935.

[20] Minutes, supra, April 15, 1937. The chapel was completed in March, 1937.

Shortly after the mission was organized, the immediate priority was the construction of a church building.[21] Efforts in this regard took the form of fund-raising projects. Cards, printed to depict the chapel to be built, were sent to Episcopal communicants in Tennessee soliciting funds for construction.[22] The building depicted on the cards by architect Lucian Dent[23] was brick and masonry with a metal roof, one of much more substantial material than the simple, frame, Victorian structure that was built.[24] While the cards were an effective project, probably the most lucrative efforts were the barbeques and parties. One such event occurred on September 28, 1934, at the

---

[21] Acklen, "Scrapbook of: History," supra. Appendix.

[22] Scruggs, "History," supra. A copy of the card is reprinted in the Appendix, Document 5.

[23] The late Lucian Minor Dent was a member of St. John's Episcopal Church of which he was also the architect. Ellen Davies Rodgers, Heirs Through Hope, supra, p. 216.

[24] While the chapel as constructed bore little similarity to the design on the cards, apparently Mr. Dent was responsible for the design of the cross.

home of Mr. and Mrs. Joseph Martin in Forest Hill.[25] It was an outdoor, evening dinner with dancing on the canvased tennis courts of "Martindale" attended by many of the socially prominent in the community.[26] The Kirbys also hosted similar fund-raising functions.[27] As a result of these activities, the monetary gifts from mission communicants and their families and friends together with that of the Episcopal Church Extension Fund[28] --the construction funds for the mission's first church building, the chapel--were gathered.

---

[25] The Commercial Appeal, September 22, 1934.

[26] In addition to the founders the ticket committee included Dr. and Mrs. Charles Blaisdell, the Reverend and Mrs. William Dubose Bratton, Mr. and Mrs. John Lippitt, Mr. and Mrs, Shubael Beasley, Mr. and Mrs. Thorton Buckner, Mr. and Mrs. Robert Bruce, Mr. and Mrs. Stanley Trezevant, Mr. and Mrs. Dabney Crump, Mr. and Mrs. P. H. Gideon, and Miss Mary G. Hutchison. Id.

[27] Interview with Dorothy K. Wills, November 29, 1983.

[28] Scruggs, "History," supra.

The congregation spent its last Christmas that year in its makeshift church in the Lodge Hall. The circumstances in which the congregation worshipped may seem a primitive and pitiful scene, but to those who were communicants, it was a miracle in progress.[29]

29
  The green kneelers in the Lodge were hand-stuffed by the ladies of the mission. Interview with Dorothy K. Wills, supra.

CORNERSTONE LAID FOR
ST. GEORGE'S EPISCOPAL MISSION

Procession from Masonic Lodge Hall to site
of New Mission to be constructed

At a service conducted by Archdeacon Charles Weller on Sunday, October 11, 1936, at four-thirty in the afternoon, the cornerstone of the Chapel of St. George's Mission was laid.[30] Assisting Archdeacon Weller were the Reverend W. E. Dakin and John B. Scruggs, layreader and members of the choir of St. John's Episcopal Church.[31] Approximately one-hundred

---

[30] Acklen, "Scrapbook History," supra.
[31] The Commercial Appeal, October 10, 1936.

ARCHDEACON CHARLES K. WELLER

persons attended the service and witnessed the laying of the cornerstone, which contained a copper box into which were placed papers of the church and diocese, a short history of the mission, lists of its officers and members, and a list of those attending the ceremony.[32]

Construction actually had begun before the service on the site directly north across Spring Street from the mission's temporary quarters in the Lodge Hall.[33] The lot as previously mentioned in the Pre-Mission Story was acquired by the Diocese in 1924 from the Strickland heirs in exchange for a lot devised to the Diocese in 1903 by W. W. Bott.[34] While it is said that the supervision was undertaken by

---

[32] Ibid.

[33] The location was on the northeast corner of Germantown Road and Spring Street. Directly west across Germantown Road at that time was "Mimosa," the estate of Col. James Hammond. The Commercial Appeal, October 10, 1936.

[34] See The Pre-Mission Story, supra.

ST. GEORGE'S CHAPEL AND CONGREGATION- OCTOBER, 1937

Hiram T. Adair and John B. Hebron, the actual work and supervision were performed by Mark Roy Finley, the contractor.[35] Work continued through the winter months until completion in March, 1937, a remarkable achievement considering the time of year. The result was a simple, frame, Victorian structure seating about eighty persons, completed debt-free at a total cost of approximately two-thousand dollars.[36]

The consecration of the Chapel of St. George's Mission took place on Easter Sunday, March 28, 1937,[37] at four o'clock in the afternoon.[38] Bishop Maxon's comments about the occasion from his diary are descriptive of the event:

---

[35] Mr. Finley was Mrs. Acklen's father. Louise Acklen, "Scrapbook History," supra.

[36] The Commercial Appeal, October 10, 1936.

[37] The consecration date of the chapel has from time to time been inaccurately reported as March 17, a date which in 1937 fell on a Wednesday.

[38] The Commercial Appeal, March 27, 1937.

After dinner at the home of Mr. and Mrs. H. E.
Buckingham, Mr. Buckingham drove me to Germantown.
There at 4:00 p.m. I consecrated the new St. George's
Church, preached, blessed a beautiful brass cross
and confirmed two persons presented by the Reverend
Dr. Tracy. I was delighted with the appearance and
furnishings of this beautiful little church, but
recently completed and paid for. So many people were
present that not more than half could get into the
building. The music was furnished by sixteen members
of Calvary Choir under direction of Mr. Steuterman
and was very fine. I was impressed with the zeal
and enthusiasm shown by the good people in bringing
forward this work.39

The consecration had been planned for late December,
1936, to coincide with Archdeacon Weller's announced
retirement on January 1, 1937.⁴⁰ Considering all the
circumstances attendant to the construction, the December completion date could have been achieved only
through Divine intervention. Only one man, Mark Roy

39
 Journal, Diocese of Tennessee, pp. 57-58. The confirmations mentioned by the bishop are not recorded in the Parish Register. A newspaper account of the event indicates those confirmed were John Robert Payne and Gladys Joyce McCaa, both of Germantown. The Commercial Appeal, March 29, 1937.
40
 The Commercial Appeal, October 12, 1936.

Finley,[41] performed the work, most probably without drawings or specifications[42] but solely from the oral directions of John Hebron and Hiram Adair. It was still rather phenomenal that the building was completed within the six-month period of uncertain weather.

From the time of its organization and for several years after the consecration of the chapel, the mission received gifts for its furnishing from individuals and local Episcopal churches. When services began in the Lodge Hall, a litany desk and lectern were given by John Scruggs.[43] Later, after being

---

[41] Mr. Finley was a devout and loyal member of the Germantown Methodist Church. Interview with Louise F. Acklen, December 23, 1983.

[42] Ibid.

[43] As a result of his position with the U.S. Corps of Engineers, John Scruggs had the shop make a litany desk and lectern. Scruggs, "History of the Mission," supra. Appendix. The altar which appears cloth-covered in photographs apparently was only a table. Interviews with Kenneth Robertson, 1982 and 1983.

refinished, these two pieces were moved into the chapel upon its completion.[44] The "beautiful brass cross" mentioned by Bishop Maxon[45] was the gift of Grace Episcopal Church, Memphis; a baptismal font was given by the Church of the Good Shepherd, Memphis.[46] The altar linen was the gift of Mamie Cloyes, who received it from her mother in Austria.[47] The most historically significant gift, a silver communion service, donated by Mrs. Ben Bruce, the former Alma

---

[44] Scruggs, "New Episcopal Mission," supra. Appendix.

[45] See Note 39, supra. This cross is now in the relocated and restored chapel and bears this inscription:
> Presented to St. George's Church
> Germantown by Grace Church
> Memphis   Christmas   1936

[46] This font, probably wooden, was later replaced by a gray granite font which is still in use.

[47] Acklen, "Scrapbook of: History," supra. Appendix.

Hanks,[48] was said to have been used by Germantown Episcopalians for forty years.[49] It represented one of the few links between that first Germantown congregation[50] and the first mission established in the community.

Five years after the mission began, a brass processional cross, which is still in use,[51] was given by the church school.[52] It replaced the plain wooden

---

[48] See Note 55, Pre-Mission Story, supra.

[49] This communion service most probably was used by that first congregation which met at the Germantown Presbyterian Church during the first two decades of this century. See notes 21, 22, 23, 24, Pre-Mission Story, supra.

[50] See Note 64, Pre-Mission Story, supra.

[51] The cross is now used as a Clergy Cross. It continued to be used as processional cross until January 1, 1984, when it was replaced by a larger St. Phillip's Cross, which was consecrated for use on January 8, 1984.

[52] The inscription indicates it was given on April 9, 1939.

crux[53] which had been used since the time the mission was quartered in the Masonic Lodge. Probably a short time thereafter, the mission received an electronic organ[54] for the chapel given by William (Bill) Terry,[55] the manager of the New York Giants Baseball Club.[56]

53
 The cross is shown at the head of a procession out of the Lodge Hall for the cornerstone laying service on October 11, 1936. The Commercial Appeal, October 12, 1936. See photograph, p. 68, supra.

54
 This gift was made probably in 1938, 1939, or possibly as late as 1940 since the Terry family were communicants for only a few years. Interviews with Dorothy K. Wills and Elisabeth Powell Hughes, January, 1984.

55
 The Terrys were communicants of the mission for several years during the late 1930's. Their home presently houses the Lichterman Nature Study Center, 5992 Quince Road, Memphis. Ibid. They transferred to St. John's Episcopal Church, Memphis, on January 1, 1941. St. George's Episcopal Church, Register 1, pp. 44-45.

56
 Mr. Terry, called "Memphis Bill" by his baseball colleagues, was manager of the New York Giants from 1932 until 1941. Britannica Junior Encyclopedia, 1975 ed., s.v. "Baseball," p. 728.

This instrument replaced a reed pump organ which had been in use, probably from the time the congregation had moved from the Masonic Lodge Hall into the chapel.[57] During those early years the mission received other less significant gifts, only some of which are mentioned in the early chronicles[58] but which contributed to the completion of the chapel as the Episcopal church in Germantown, Tennessee.

---

[57] Before the pump organ, the congregation used a piano while quartered in the Lodge Hall. Interviews with Louise Acklen Rosengarten and Elisabeth Powell Hughes, January, 1984.

[58] See Scruggs, "New Episcopal Mission," supra; Acklen, "Scrapbook of: History," supra. Appendix.

CHAPEL AFTER COMPLETION-1938

The Mission Clergy 79

During the more than two and one-half years that the congregation of the mission met in the Germantown Masonic Lodge Hall, Archdeacon Weller, the priest-in-charge, was present on only the third Sunday of each month to celebrate Holy Communion and preach.[59] There is some indication, however, that Archdeacon Weller devoted more time to the new mission of St. George's than he did to St. Andrew's or any of the other missions with which he was charged.[60] During those early years when no priest was present, the mission layreader, John Scruggs, conducted morning prayer services and was obliged to deliver the layman's sermon. There seemed little question as to which was his favorite. Some early communicants remember hearing one particular layreader sermon on the Old Testament heroes, Shadrach, Meshach and Abednego,[61]

---

[59] Acklen, "Scrapbook of: History," supra. Appendix.
[60] He reported that during the year 1935 he attempted to hold only one preaching mission, that in the new mission of St. George's, Germantown. Journal, 1936, p.101.
[61] Daniel 3 (King James).

on more than one occasion.[62]

With the consecration of the chapel in March, 1937, Bishop Maxon assigned Dr. Sterling Tracy as Deacon-in-charge of the mission.[63] It should be remembered that any clergyman at the new mission was then assigned on a part-time basis only. He was required to divide his time among several missions in the area and other diocesan duties.

The Reverend Dr. Tracy served only a short time, for in 1938 the very Reverend Harold Hoag was indicated as priest-in-charge of the mission.[64] As dean of

---

[62] Mr. Scruggs apparently was very fond of this sermon and read it on more occasions than the congregation desired to hear it. Interviews with Thomas L. Phillips, Virginia Phillips, and Kenneth Robertson, December, 1983.

[63] Diocesan Archives, St. Mary's Cathedral, Memphis, Tennessee, Parochial Report of St. George's Mission, 1937; Dr. Tracy had been ordained a deacon only the previous January. The Commercial Appeal, March 27, 1937.

[64] Diocesan Archives, supra, Parochial Report of St. George's Misson, 1938. However, Thomas P. Simpson is shown as priest-in-charge in 1938 by the Diocesan Journal. Journal, 1939, p. 117.

the cathedral, he was probably unable to devote much time to the mission.[65] Consequently, from 1938 to 1940 both the Reverend Mr. David Rose and the Reverend Mr. Thomas Simpson appeared at the mission as supply clergy for the dean.[66] Like most rural missions during this period, the congregation saw a priest only one Sunday a month for the celebration of Holy Communion.

As the decade drew to a close and the mission began to grow,[67] the congregation desired a resident

---

[65] While early communicants do remember Dr. Sterling Tracy and other supply clergy, they have no recollection of Dean Hoag's visitations to the mission. Interviews with Kenneth Robertson and Louise Acklen Rosengarten, January, 1984, and February, 1984.

[66] Both together with Archdeacon Weller, Dr. Tracy, and the Reverend Mr. Guy Usher are indicated in the mission registers as rectors. Obviously, their names entered only as early clergy of the mission. St. George's Episcopal Church, Register , p. 37.

[67] From seventeen communicants with a budget of $131.43 in 1934 the mission had grown to forty-six communicants with a budget of $1,506.76 by the end of 1940. Diocesan Archives, supra, Parochial Reports of St. George's Mission, 1934, 1940.

priest-in-charge even if his time had to be shared with other missions. As a result the wardens of the mission, John Hebron and Carl Graves, met with both diocesan bishops in September, 1939, to persuade them to assign a priest to be a resident at Germantown.[68] After their meeting, as a coincidence, the bishop co-adjutor met with the Reverend Mr. Guy S. Usher.[69] The bishops promised to assign a resident priest the following year; however, as a consideration, the mission was required to undertake an increase in its contribution to stipend, apportionment, and assessment from $200.00 to $1,200.00 per year.[70] The bishops made good their promise by sending Mr. Usher to be resident in Germantown at St. George's Mission

---

[68] The wardens met at eight the evening of September 17, 1939, with the bishops. The coadjutor's diary indicates the meeting was with regard to the mission's becoming a parish; however, the diocesan publication Forward in Tennessee reported that it was for the purpose of placing a resident minister at Germantown. Journal, 1940, p. 104; Forward in Tennessee, November, 1939.

[69] Journal, 1940, p. 104.

[70] Forward in Tennessee, supra.

in charge also of St. Andrew's in Collierville and St. Ann's in Woodstock.[71] The congregation of the mission made a good-faith effort to fulfill its part of the bargain, but it is doubtful that it did since the total budget for 1940 was $1,506.76.[72] Considering the economic conditions at that time, the little congregation performed a phenomenal task of more than doubling the budget in one year,[73] which apparently satisfied the bishops since a priest remained resident at Germantown until the mission achieved parish status in 1944, except for a two-month period in 1941.[74]

With the presence of clergy resident at the mission the congregation began to feel as though they

---

[71] Journal, p. 128.

[72] Diocesan Archives, supra, Parochial Reports of St. George's Mission, 1940.

[73] Ibid., 1939, 1940.

[74] Ibid., 1941.

had truly become a church.[75] This mood probably caused others in later years incorrectly to recite that parish status had been achieved in 1940.[76] That status was not accomplished for several years after the Reverend Mr. Guy Usher had left the mission. Although he was resident at St. George's a year only, his presence was obviously one of the reasons the congregation more than doubled in that one year.[77] Perhaps another factor was the preaching mission held at St. George's during the second week in April, 1940,

---

[75] With the presence of resident clergy for the first time since 1934, it is most probable that the register of the misson was for the first time put into order. See Sources, infra. Appendix.

[76] The year 1940 has been cited in numerous publications, letters, and other documents including some authored by this writer (in ignorance) as the year parish status was achieved. It has also been incorrectly stated as the year of parish status by Mrs. Rogers in her book, The Romance of the Episcopal Church in West Tennessee on p. 186. See note 38, Pre-Mission Story, supra.

[77] Diocesan Archives, supra, Parochial Reports of St. George's Mission, 1940, 1941.

by the bishop coadjutor.[78] Bishop Dandridge spent the entire week in the Germantown "field," as it was called, with the preaching mission at St. George's and visitations to St. Andrew's and St. Ann's, then at Woodstock, Tennessee.[79]

With the resignation of the Reverend Mr, Usher in late 1940 the mission gave its first resident priest to an old Memphis parish which had fallen on hard times.[80] Mr. Usher became priest-in-charge of that parish, Church of the Good Shepherd, on January 1, 1941.[81] Even before the Reverend Mr. Usher left, the wardens and vestry met with the bishop coadjutor

---

[78] Journal, 1941, p. 96.

[79] Ibid.

[80] The Church of the Good Shepherd was formally reduced to an aided parish from a full parish on January 21, 1942, by the Convention. Journal, 1942, p. 28.

[81] At that time the Church of the Good Shepherd was located at Fourth and Mill in Memphis, to which location the Reverend Mr. Usher was assigned. Ibid., p. 134.

regarding a successor as priest-in-charge of the mission.[82] The mission's layleaders were not about to permit the fruits of the efforts of the past year to be wasted by a decline in interest by the congregation because of the absence of resident clergy. Therefore they met with the bishop coadjutor on December 20, 1940, with reference to a successor to the Reverend Mr. Usher.[83] As a result the Reverend Mr. Charles Widney became the priest-in-charge at Germantown[84] with St. George's in the care of its second resident priest.

Unlike the Reverend Mr. Usher, who had been ordained only a short time before his assignment to St. George's,[85] the Reverend Charles Leonidas Widney

---

[82] Journal, 1941, p. 106.

[83] Ibid., p. 106.

[84] With the assignment of the Reverend Mr. Guy Usher to be resident at Germantown, it became known as "the Germantown field," including not only St. George's but also St. Andrew's in Collierville and St. Ann's in Woodstock, Journal, 1942, p. 8.

[85] The Reverend Mr. Guy Samuel Usher was ordained to the priesthood in January, 1939. Journal, 1940, p. 63.

had served several churches during his more than ten-year priesthood. He came to St. George's from Otey Memorial Chapel in Sewanee, Tennessee. It was during the period that the Reverend Mr. Widney was priest-in-charge of the mission that the congregation reached a peak of 110 communicants.[86] This status occurred in 1942 with a subsequent decline during the years of World War II, for it was not until 1946 that the

---

[86] Diocesan Archives, supra, Parochial Reports of St. George's Mission, 1942.

THE REVEREND CHARLES L. WIDNEY

number of communicants exceeded the peak achieved in 1942.[87] Obviously, the stagnation in growth during those years resulted from effects of the war,[88] but even so during that period the mission achieved the economic self-sufficiency needed to become a parish.

---

[87] Ibid., 1946.

[88] The budget actually increased in 1943 and 1944 with fewer communicants. Ibid., 1943, 1944.

THE REVEREND GUY S. USHER
PHOTOGRAPH, 1982

THE EARLY PARISH

When the Reverend Charles Widney became the resident priest-in-charge at St. George's, the wardens of the mission had learned full well the importance of resident clergy to the continued growth of the mission. Therefore it was not unusual that the Ladies Auxiliary of the mission welcomed the Reverend Mr. Widney and his wife at a tea on St. George's Day in 1941.[1] The setting for the occasion was the home of Colonel and Mrs. James Hammond, located a short distance south of the chapel on Germantown Road.[2] More than two-hundred Episcopalians were invited to the affair at which the diocesan bishop and his wife joined in receiving the guests.[3] The Reverend Mr. Widney, who formally began his duties as priest-in-

---

[1] The tea complimenting the Widneys was held from four to six on the afternoon of April 23, 1941. The Commercial Appeal, April 19, 1941.

[2] The Hammonds were communicants of the mission; their home, "Mimosa," was set off Germantown Road with a drive lined with mimosa trees.

[3] The Commercial Appeal, supra. Also see Episcopal Churchwomen, Appendix.

charge on March, 1941,[4] was obviously impressed by the warm reception he received at the mission. Less than three years later, as resident priest of St. George's with the care of missions at Collierville and Woodstock, the Reverend Charles Widney became the first Rector of St. George's Parish. The Articles of Association of St. George's Parish, the prerequisite to admission as a parish to the Convention, was apparently prepared by Carl Graves and signed by many of the communicants of the mission.[6] On Thursday, January 30, 1944, upon the motion of the Reverend Paul E. Sloan for the Committee on Status of Parishes and Missions, St. George's Church was admitted to union with the Convention as a parish.[7] With the attainment of parish status the congregation was no longer dependent

---

[4] St. George's Episcopal Church, Register 1, p. 37.

[5] See note 7, infra. There are no extant vestry minutes to confirm the Reverend Mr. Widney's call.

[6] The legal-sized document cover bore the label "Ballon, Graves & Nicholson, Attorneys-at-Law, Porter Building, Memphis, Tenn." See Document 10, Appendix.

[7] Journal, Diocese of Tennessee, 1944, p. 34.

on the diocese for clergy, but it became responsible to support its clergy financially. Thus also ended St. George's ten-year relationship with the sister missions of St. Ann's and St. Andrew's.[8]

The Parish Begins to Grow

As World War II drew to a close, the young parish experienced growing pains because of the war effort. During its first few years of existence the mission had relatively few young children in the congregation.[9] During the mission years and for several years after St. George's became a parish, the Masonic Lodge Hall was again used by the congregation for

---

[8] In addition to sharing common clergy, the communicants of St. George's and St. Andrew's had been especially close. Even as late as 1950 children from St. Andrew's attended church school at St. George's. Interview with Helen O'Brien, March 28, 1984. On October 29, 1950, the two congregations participated in a joint service. St. George's Episcopal Church, Vestry Minutes, October 9, 1950.

[9] Interviews with Kenneth Robertson and Louise Acklen, 1984.

for church school school.[10] The need for church-school facilities was met in 1947 by an addition to the chapel of two school rooms and a vestry room.[11] A rectory was constructed on a lot owned by the parish south of the Masonic Lodge Hall[12] during 1945 and 1946, approximately a year prior to the chapel addition.[13] In the year in which the new schoolrooms were completed, the church-school attendance more than doubled.[14]

The years following the parish's first major expansion of its physical facilities saw a continued

---

[10] Interviews with Kenneth Robertson and Helen O'Brien, supra.

[11] Diocesan Archives, St. Mary's Cathedral, Memphis, Tennessee, Parochial Reports of St. George's Parish, 1945, 1946.

[12] The new rectory was later designated as 2602 South Germantown Road and still stands at this writing.

[13] Diocesan Archives, supra. Parochial Reports of St. George's Parish, 1945, 1946, 1947.

[14] From 29 in 1945 to 50 after 1946 and to 60 in 1947. Ibid.

but rather slow growth.[15] During the period between 1947 and 1950 there appeared little change in the budget or the number of communicants.[16] In 1949 there did occur a significant esthetic improvement in the chapel with the installation of stained glass windows replacing the original windows. They were offered as a gift to the parish by Mr. and Mrs. Jere L. Crook;[17] however, the offer was either not accepted by the vestry, or it was withdrawn.[18] The women of the parish through various fund-raising activities were

---

[15] Diocesan Archives, supra, Parochial Reports of St. George's Parish, 1947-1950.

[16] The period reflected no increase in the budget and only seven additional communicants. Ibid.

[17] The minutes of the vestry meeting on the night of January 14, 1949, at the home of Winston Cheairs indicate that the offer by the Crooks was accepted, but, in fact, it seems that there occurred a very heated discussion. Several members of the vestry felt that other priorities were in order, one of which was the steps on the west side of the chapel which seemed in constant need of repair. Interview with Kenneth Robertson and Helen O'Brien, supra.

[18] It seems more probable to the author that the gift was not accepted. Mr. Crook continued to attend almost all of the vestry meetings until his resignation in November, 1949, as a result of his transfer to Calvary Church, Memphis. Vestry Minutes, November 14, 1949.

primarily responsible for the purchase and installation of the windows.[19] In the same year another welcomed improvement came with the installation of an attic fan,[20] which in those days was about the only respite from the heat in the summer.

Those early parish years were difficult financially, even though by that time St. George's had its share of affluent members.[21] During those early years the parish had a number of members who had quite substantial fiscal capabilities that were not reflected in their support of the parish.[22] There

---

[19] Interviews with Dorothy Robertson, Helen O'Brien, and Kenneth Robertson, supra. Also see Episcopal Churchwomen, Appendix.

[20] The fan was donated by Mrs. Walter May. St. George's Episcopal Church, Vestry Minutes, May 19, 1949; June 13, 1949.

[21] Interview with Kenneth Robertson, supra.

[22] Ibid.

were two members,[23] both of whom were frequent vestry members, who individually from year to year supplemented the budget to prevent deficits.[24] The continuing financial problem had its greatest effect on the rector and his family as their needs increased.[25] It was not surprising, therefore, that the Reverend Mr. Widney resigned in April, 1952.[26] At the regular monthly vestry meeting preceding the resignation, the rector's salary and auto allowance were referred to the budget committee for consideration.[27] At a special called meeting of the vestry on March 16, 1952, the budget including the rector's salary was approved. Apparently, the vestry's efforts did not satisfy what Mr. Widney felt were his needs since his

---

[23] Frank King, Sr., and Raymond C. Firestone. Ibid. Raymond Christy Firestone, one of the Firestone brothers, was a member of St. George's from 1945 until 1949. St. George's Episcopal Church, Register No.1, pp. 54-55.

[24] Interview with Kenneth Robertson, supra.

[25] Ibid.

[26] Minutes, April 14, 1952.

[27] Minutes, March 10, 1952.

resignation was announced at the following monthly vestry meeting.

At the same vestry meeting the senior warden appointed a committee [29] to confer with the bishop about the calling of a new rector from eligible clergy. Subsequently, in May the vestry met with Bishop Barth and found his suggested replacement to be an attractive candidate.[30] Less than a month later the vestry requested the bishop for the services of Mr. Thomas A.

---

[28] Minutes, April 14, 1952. It is significant that the rector's stipend in 1950 and 1951 amounted to only about $2,500.00 per year, whereas the vestry approved $4,200.00 per year for the new rector. Minutes, June 9, 1952.

[29] The committee was composed of Charles Kortrecht, Chairman; J. T. Jones, Jr.; Frank King, Jr.; and James W. O'Brien. Ibid.

[30] This meeting probably occurred on May 18, 1952, when Bishop Barth visited. Journal, 1953, p. 94.

Roberts.[31] The vestry could not formally call Mr. Roberts since he was at that time still only a candidate for holy orders, having recently completed seminary. Since it was the bishop who had initially proposed Mr. Roberts,[32] his approval was only a formality.

---

[31] Minutes, May 12, 1952. A penciled annotation to the vestry minutes of May 12, 1952, indicates that Mr. Roberts visited St. George's on two occasions before the vestry requested his services. Minutes, May 12, 1952.

[32] Interview with Kenneth Robertson, supra.

A NEW BEGINNING

The Reverend Thomas Adams Roberts and his family[1] arrived at St. George's only days after he had been ordained to the diaconate,[2] formally beginning his duties on August 31, 1952.[3] The Reverend Mr. Roberts was obviously not bashful, for one of his first requests was to be accorded the privileges of a rector,[4] though he had been ordained a deacon less than a month. He almost immediately set about expressing views, attitudes and objectives regarding the various aspects of the parish. Clearly a man of mature judgment, Mr. Roberts postponed suggestions of change, such as "revising" the altar,[5] until other

---

[1] The Reverend Mr. Roberts came with his wife, Josephyne, and young children, Tom Junior and a daughter, Jody.

[2] The ordination took place on August 21, 1952, at the Church of the Good Shepherd, Lookout Mountain, Tennessee. Journal, 1953, p. 101.

[3] He arrived sometime before a conference with Bishop Barth on August 25, 1952, in Memphis. Ibid., p. 102.

[4] Minutes, September 8, 1952.

[5] Minutes, October 13, 1952. His purpose was to wait for reaction.

financial commitments were satisfied. Another change was quietly imposed by the vestry when the church school fund was absorbed into the General Fund of the parish.[6] For the first time the church school budget would become part of the parish's budget, for it had been operated independently since the congregation had begun as a mission.[7]

---

[6] Ibid.
[7] Interview with Kenneth Robertson, April 10, 1984.

THE REVEREND THOMAS A. ROBERTS

The vestry, the rector, and many parishioners were keenly aware of the woefully inadequate facilities of the parish with its growing congregation. After the annual Parish Meeting on January 15, 1953, a special called meeting of the vestry took place at which the Reverend Mr. Roberts announced that the Phillip Winston family were leaving Germantown and their property on Highway 72 would be on the market.[8] The vestry gave the Reverend Mr. Roberts authority to appear before the Bishop and Council for permission to obtain a thirty-day option on the property.[9] No doubt the minute entry recorded only one part of the transaction, since the Bishop and Council authorization would not have been required for an option.[10] In fact, the Bishop and Council's action was intended to permit an increase in the amount of the indebtedness on the

---

[8] Minutes, January 18, 1955.
[9] Ibid.
[10] Interview with Charles M. Crump, April 11, 1984.

101

Construction of Winston Home and Shop

parish's existing property.[11] Later, the Convention by resolution authorized the sale of the existing parish property, the purchase of a new site, and the placing of a mortgage on same in an amount sufficient to defray the balance of the purchase price of the new property.[12] With the requisite diocesan approval completed, the vestry immediately set about marshalling the assets of the parish and making plans necessary to finance the bold, new venture. A planning committee organized to spearhead the efforts to finance the venture was formed,[13] one of the duties of which was to make an inventory of the real estate owned

---

[11] The Reverend Mr. Roberts and Mr. Dunbar Abston appeared before the Bishop and Council to request its consent. Journal, 1954, p. 139.

[12] Mr. Gale for the Committee on Finance and Assessments proposed the resolution, which was approved on January 22, 1955. Journal, 1953, pp. 30-31.

[13] The committee was composed of vestrymen Dunbar Abston and Winston Cheairs. Other communicant members were Vance Alexander, Everett Cook, and E. H. Sanders. Minutes, February 9, 1953.

by the parish and the approximate value of same.[14]
Initially, the committee's purpose was to determine
the financial feasibility of the plan to move the
location of the parish.[15] Once this plan had been
determined favorable, efforts began to market separately each of the properties owned by the parish.
It became all too apparent, however, that disposition
of the chapel would be difficult.[16] As a result a
proposal was made to the Winstons that in exchange for
their property[17] they receive the chapel and the sum

---

[14]
 Mr. Abston reported that the church building was valued at between $10,000.00 and $12,000.00 as a church, the rectory with lot at between $15,000.00 and $16,000.00, and several lots east and south of the Masonic Lodge Hall at $1,000.00 each. Minutes, February 9, 1953.

[15]
 Ibid.

[16]
 Ibid.

[17]
 The Winstons had purchased the approximately twenty-acre tract only a few years earlier from Jere L. Crook and Janie P. Crook and had constructed the building, which became their home and workshop. Interview by correspondence with Virginia (Winston) McDonough, December, 1983.

of $40,000.00.[18] The Winstons accepted the offer,[19] and the vestry then proceeded with a building-fund campaign, which continued into 1954.[20]

While the vestry included many men of ability and vision, the leadership of the clergy was also extraordinary. The Reverend Mr. Roberts was still only a deacon-in-training, for his ordination to the priesthood did not take place until February 28, 1953.[21] While he had been successful in business before his call to the ministry,[22] he still was only fresh out of

---

[18] Minutes, February 9, 1953.

[19] The Winstons, who had been members of the parish only a short time, both participated in the property exchange, even though the tract was titled only in Mrs. Winston's name. Register's Office, Shelby County, Tennessee, Book 2726, p. 580.

[20] Minutes, March 9, 1953. A brochure was prepared depicting the new church to aid in obtaining building-fund pledges. Ibid.

[21] The service took place at St. Mary's Cathedral, Memphis, Journal, Diocese of Tennessee, 1954, p. 83. See Document 14, Appendix.

[22] The Reverend Mr. Roberts had been general manager of the M.M. Hedges Mfg. Co. in Chattanooga from 1943 until 1950, when he entered the seminary. Interview by correspondence with Josephyne R. Spruill, January, 1984.

seminary when he undertook with the vestry to move the location of the parish. His leadership qualities were apparently convincing to a vestry whose membership was generally older,[23] for it unanimously voted to call him as the parish's second rector immediately upon his ordination.[24]

After pausing for the ordination, the new rector and vestry launched into the problems attendant to disposing of the parish properties and financing the venture.[25] One of the financing obstacles which required solution was the consent of the Equitable Life Assurance Society, the mortgage holder on the Winston property, to the transfer of the property and the assumption of the indebtedness by the parish.[26] This

---

[23] He was only thirty-four when he became rector. Ibid.
[24] Minutes, February 9, 1953.
[25] Minutes, March 9, 1953.
[26] Minutes, April 6, 1953; Dennis W. Dean to E. M. Barber, April 17, 1953, St. George's Episcopal Church Records.

task was undertaken and successfully accomplished by one of the vestrymen, Dennis Dean.[27] Vestryman Dunbar Abston was authorized to list the remaining church properties with the E. H. Crump Company for sale and handle the matter in his discretion.[28] The building-fund campaign became the responsibility of Ed Dillard.[29] At the same vestry meeting in April, 1953, the Reverend Mr. Roberts announced a "very hot prospect" for the purchase of "the church property."[30]

---

[27] Ibid. Interviews with Kenneth Robertson and Otto Lyons, Arpil, 1984.

[28] While the minute entry so states, it was implied by later vestry action that any sale was subject to vestry approval, however; see note 31, infra.

[29] Minutes, April 6, 1953.

[30] The vestry minutes are vague when referring to the various church properties. Ibid.

This property was not the chapel, since it had been previously obligated to the Winstons, but the rectory, for which on April 30, 1953, a contract of sale[31] was concluded.[32]

On June 11, 1953, title to the Winston tract of almost twenty acres between U. S. Highway 72 and Dogwood Road passed to St. George's Episcopal Church.[33] Prior to this time, the congregation evidently had possession of the premises, for a picnic barbeque was held on St. George's Day.[34] Also, an architect had been retained, and some initial work had been begun

---

[31] Either there was no May vestry meeting or it was not recorded as indicating approval of the sale of the rectory. See note 28, supra.

[32] Franklin Ruegsegger and his wife, Ann, purchased the rectory for #13,500.00. Records, supra. The closing was delayed until July 24, 1953, because of loan commitment problems. Records, supra.

[33] Register's Office, Shelby County, Tennessee, Book 3178, p. 551.

[34] April 23, 1953. Minutes, April 6, 1953.

by parish members.[35] During this period the chapel remained in use since the building at the new site was still in the process of alteration. Consequently, the parish began making monthly rental payments for the use of the chapel in June.[36] The chapel continued to be used until late August[37] when the congregation moved to the new building.[38]

---

[35] Ibid. Minutes, March 9, 1953.

[36] The vestry authorized payment of $100.00 per month commencing June 1, 1953. Minutes, June 8, 1953.

[37] Interview with Kenneth Robertson, April 18, 1984.

[38] The move was made several days before Sunday, August 30, 1953. Ibid. The rector and his family moved into the rectory of the new building sometime in July, 1953, since the contract of sale of the former rectory provided for possession on July 24, 1953, the closing date. See note 32, supra.

109

St. George's Altar as
it Appeared in November, 1953

The Altar as it Appeared
after Completion

On Thursday evening, August 27th, the men of the parish sponsored a benefit barbeque supper on the grounds of the new church.[39] The event was planned to offer those attending an opportunity to inspect the new church and to raise funds for Sunday school rooms on the second floor of the building.[40] The following Sunday, August 30, 1953, the congregation of the parish attended the first service held in the second sanctuary of St. George's Episcopal Church.[41] Although renovation was still continuing, the construction at the east end of the building was completed enough so that services could be held.[42] The renovation work during that summer that was performed

---

[39] *The Collierville Herald*, August 20, 1953, p. 1.

[40] Ibid. The vestry minutes indicate only that a "picnic" was to be held on August 27th; the net profit from it was $1,884.25. Minutes, August 10, 1953, September 14, 1953.

[41] *The Collierville Herald*, supra. No mention of the first service is made in the vestry minutes or in the Memphis newspapers.

[42] The church sanctuary occupied the east half of the ground floor and the rectory the west half of the building. Records, supra.

by a number of parishioners with the rector provided a fellowship of labor which drew them close together as they achieved their common goal.[43] The experience of that summer made lifelong friendships, some of which still continue.[44]

After the sanctuary was substantially completed, efforts were focused on the completion of space for Sunday school and other parish activities on the second floor of the building above the rectory.[45] At that time the rectory, formerly the Winstons' living quarters, occupied the west half of the building; above it was a large, open area which was converted into a parish hall, kitchen, bathroom, and a bedroom in the northwest corner near the staircase.[46] Sunday

---

[43] Interview with Ednamae Thompson, April 19, 1984.
[44] Ibid.
[45] Ibid.
[46] The bedroom was part of the rectory occupied by the Roberts' son, Thomas. Interview with Kenneth Robertson, Ednamae Thompson, Helen O'Brien, supra.

school classes were conducted in the parish hall area through the use of portable partitions.[47] Completion of this part of the building was delayed until mid-1954 when the exterior work was begun by the contractor,[48] even though much work had been performed during the interim by members of the parish.

Shortly after the parish had moved into its new, remodeled home, the rector and the vestry soon discovered the increased needs of a larger church and grounds. Not only the most elemental items such as additional prayer books and hymnals were required,[49] but a much larger building and grounds almost twenty

---

[47] This area probably was not completed until late 1954 by the contractor who performed the exterior construction. Ibid. Louise F. Acklen, "Scrapbook of St. George's Episcopal Church" (1965), Appendix.

[48] The construction completing this area of the building also included the contract for the entrance. See note 52, infra.

[49] Minutes, October 12, 1953.

times larger demanded maintenance.[50]

The year 1954 saw the realization of the initial plans for the parish's new home on the hill east of Germantown.[51] In June the vestry authorized construction of the entrance[52] to the church building as well as other interior work.[53] Initially, a tower[54] to be centered on the south side of the building was proposed; however, the plan was revised because of the

---

[50] While it probably was not necessary at that time to maintain the entire tract, the area around the church building was substantially larger than the former site. Ibid.

[51] The new site was approximately one mile east of the Germantown corporate limits.

[52] The architects, Windrom, Haglund and Venable, recommended the low bidder, Conner and Boucher, as contractor. Minutes, June-July, 1954. The contract was signed June 14, 1954. Records, supra.

[53] See note 48, supra. Also see Document 12, Appendix.

[54] The proposed tower is depicted in a newspaper photograph found in Mrs. Acklen's "Scrapbook." Appendix.

cost of such a structure.[55] A revised plan calling for a simple steeple in the center of the building with a gabled entrance on the south at the center of the building was apparently further revised to exclude the steeple.[56] The final entrance plan approved consisted of a gabled south narthex addition in the center of the building with a cross ensconced over the doorway.[57] After 1954 the next major construction took place inside the building, when the

---

[55] One unidentified plan had an estimated cost of $10,000.00. Minutes, March 8, 1953. The final plan was approved at a price of $7,800.00. Minutes, June-July, 1953.

[56] Records, supra.

[57] Minutes, June-July, 1953. Tha actual contract price was $7,700.00 Records, supra. See photograph below.

Entrance of New Church Building

Reverend Frank McClain had become rector, and the rectory was moved to the remodeled tenant house east of the main building.[58]

As the first twenty years of the parish's existence drew to a close, construction continued on the facilities at the new location. In the last two years of that period, through the dynamic leadership of the rector supported by an aggressive vestry, the parish had achieved that which few would have dreamed only several years earlier. It was not accomplished, however, without risk, for there was a substantial indebtedness considering the size of the congregation,[59] but the stage was set for growth and what was to become one of the major Episcopal churches in the diocese.

---

[58] The tenant house has been known through the years as the "chicken coop" and "the little red schoolhouse."

[59] By November, 1955, the debt had been reduced to only $25,000.00. The vestry to the communicants, November 21, 1955, Document 17, Appendix.

Epilogue

The Reverend Mr. Roberts, a dynamic and popular rector, remained at St. George's until October, 1956, when he accepted a call from Christ Church, Greenville, South Carolina. During his rectorate the parish experienced a communicant growth from 100 in 1952 to 173 by the end of 1956, Mr. Roberts' last year as rector. After his resignation the vestry called a scholarly young priest who had only a short time before become the first rector of St. Andrew's in Harriman, Tennessee.

The Reverend Frank M. McClain came to St. George's from St. Andrew's in June, 1957. Before his arrival the tenant house, which was intended to be converted into a study for the former rector, was instead converted into a rectory for the new rector. Later, during the Reverend Mr. McClain's rectorate, the rectory at the west end of the main building was converted into a small office for the rector and secretary with the remaining space for church and day school purposes.

As the parish grew, its ministry was directed in

a different direction--toward elementary education.
It was the idea and support of Eric and Margaret
Catmur, Dr. Steve Bledsoe, Joan Cowan, and others
that moved the Reverend Mr. McClain to spearhead the
creation of a school on the church grounds. St.
George's Day School began in the fall of 1959, using
the church-school facilities and part of the former
rectory. As the needs of the day school increased,
work began in June, 1961, on a six-classroom building
which was completed for dedication in February, 1962,
bearing the name of the rector. The parish had
grown to 259 communicants when Mr. McClain resigned in
1962 to accept a position at Sweetbriar College in
Virginia.

In July, 1962, the vestry voted to call the Reverend David E. Babin, who at that time was an assistant at St. John's in Knoxville. After accepting the call to become the fourth rector of St. George's, he and his family pointed out the parish's need for an adequate rectory. The remodeled tenant house east of the main building had been adequate for Mr. McClain, who was unmarried when he had become rector. The building had even been sufficient for a married couple, after Mr. McClain's marriage. It was not adequate, however, for a family with several children. In response to this need, a rectory was completed in the fall of 1964 on the north side of the church property facing Dogwood Road.

When Mr. Babin resigned in March, 1965, to accept a teaching position at Seabury-Western Theological Seminary in Illinois, the parish had grown to 279 communicants, but a more dramatic growth was seen in the church school to a total attendance of 247.

The call of the vestry in June, 1965, was accepted by the Reverend Mr. Robert Cherry, who came from Columbia, South Carolina. It was during the Reverend Mr. Cherry's rectorate in 1966 that the former rectory at the west end of the main building, part of which had been used by the day school, was converted into church offices and choir rooms with a portion used to enlarge the church and add a balcony. With this construction the church sanctuary essentially remained the same until its conversion into a parish hall in 1979. Mr. Cherry remained at St. George's less than two years when he resigned as rector in December, 1966, effective on January 1, 1967.

A new rector accepted the vestry's call in March, 1967, and arrived in April, 1967. The Reverend Sidney G. Ellis, an Englishman, came to St. George's at a time when there was considerable controversy within the church because of the policies of the National Church. Notwithstanding those problems, both church and day school continued to grow in ministry under his leadership. The need of the parish for a more adequate parish hall facility and the school for a gymnasium was met in 1967, when through the joint efforts of the parish and school construction began on a parish hall-gymnasium and two large schoolrooms. Then, in 1970 the day-school facilities were doubled with the construction of another six-classroom building adjacent to the original on the east.

By 1971 the parish had grown to 475 communicants with a church-school attendance of 294. Feeling that St. George's needed a "younger man" as rector, Mr. Ellis resigned in June, 1971. Turning again to the task of finding a new rector, the vestry in August called St. George's seventh rector, the Reverend C. Allen Cooke, the rector of St. Andrew's in Maryville, Tennessee.

The new rector, a native Memphian, arrived in September, 1971, and almost immediately began efforts to establish a closer relationship between the congregation and himself. He announced formation of a couples' group for Christian fellowship to meet once a month with a potluck supper and a cocktail period. The popularity of this idea grew as this monthly gathering, called Lancers, became one of St. George's important social activities. At the same time the 9:30 A.M. Sunday morning service was eliminated, leaving only the 7:30 A.M. communion service and the 10:30 A.M. worship service. This alteration was an effort to unify the congregation, which was still relatively small for three Sunday services. Next, the Reverend Mr. Cooke undertook to rebuild the Christian education program. When he arrived in August, 1971, the Sunday school was in a state of decline, and only one adult class existed. Within the next few years Sunday school enrollment had increased, and several adult classes were being offered. Then in 1978 the Reverend Mr. George C. Gibson became the Director of Christian Education. Through his leadership adult Christian education has grown in variety and quality during the past five years.

Several years after the Reverend Mr. Cooke became rector, Germantown experienced a population explosion which resulted in a rapid communicant growth. It was clear by 1976 the the parish needed a larger sanctuary. Therefore, the vestry undertook a building program which culminated in the third church building for the congregation. Vestry action began in 1976, and the first service in the sanctuary was held on February 18, 1979. The new building, which seats 450, was consecrated by Bishop William E. Sanders on March 4, 1979. By the end of 1980 the communicants numbered 707, and the total baptised persons 961. The budget in that year had grown to over $265,000.00.

With additional communicants and increased church operations, the need for additional clergy became apparent. In December, 1980, the vestry authorized the employment of an assistant rector and adopted a budget for the year 1981 to meet that need. The Reverend James W. Cubine, who preferred to be addressed as "Jamie," came to St. George's as a deacon-in-training on July 1, 1981, and was ordained to the priesthood on May 17, 1982, at which time he became St. George's first assistant rector. Under the Reverend Mr. Cubine's leadership, the Episcopal Young Churchmen group was revitalized in organization and in the number of its activities.

Meanwhile, the Reverend Mr. Cooke approached his tenth year at St. George's and the twenty-fifth anniversary of his ordination to the diaconate. At the initial suggestion of the Reverend Mr. Gibson, the congregation of the parish gave the Reverend Mr. Cooke and Mrs. Cooke a Festal Evensong service on May 17, 1981, in thanksgiving for their ministry. At a reception for them after the service, they were presented with an expense-paid trip to Canterbury, England.

It had been the dream of Mr. Cooke for some years after he had come to St. George's to have the chapel, the original church building, moved to the "hill" and restored. During the period from 1954 to the end of 1980, the building located immediately west of the Germantown Presbyterian Church had been used as the Germantown Library and Community Theater. In November of 1982 the building was offered for removal to St. George's by the Germantown Presbyterian Church, the owner. After a rather brief fund-raising program, the building was moved on April 10, 1981, to its new site west of the parish hall (second church building) on the same axis with the church sanctuary completed in 1979. Renovation and restoration of the chapel building continued through April, 1983. On April 23, 1982, St. George's Day, the cornerstone was laid with the original copper box sealed therein again with a history of the building, lists of members of the congregation and clergy, and a copy of the New Testament. The chapel was consecrated on June 15, 1983, by Bishop Alex D. Dickson; it became the first consecration in the new Diocese of West Tennessee.

In December, 1983, the Reverend Mr. Cubine resigned to return to private business, retaining his Holy Orders and continuing to act as a supply priest in the diocese. The Reverend Mr. Mark K. Wilson came to St. George's in March, 1984, as assistant rector from Covington, Tennessee, where he had been rector of St. Matthew's.

During 1984 new kitchen facilities were constructed in the parish hall to facilitate the preparation of meals and receptions for the congregation.

Since it began as a mission fifty years ago, the congregation of St. George's appears to have undergone several distinct changes in personality. During the first ten years while a mission, the church possessed a definite rural, country atmosphere. This tone began slowly to change after the congregation moved to the "hill" in 1953. As Germantown began to grow and to urbanize, likewise did the congregation. With the dramatic population influx during the ten-year period preceding this writing the congregation has completed the urbanization process but has also become more transient in character.

In this fiftieth year the parish is witnessing some of the same problems that were present in the early 1950's before the change in location. Except for the sanctuary, the physical facilities including the day school are more than ten years old and provide inadequate space for administrative service and Christian education activities. These problems are being met at this writing by the Long Range Planning Committee and the vestry with a view to forthcoming action to satisfy the present and future need of the parish.

At the end of its forty-ninth year the parish had grown to 780 communicants and 1,115 baptised persons. The church-school attendance had grown to 435 and, at this writing, continues a dynamic growth.

St. George's on its fiftieth anniversary is the fifth largest parish in the new Diocese of West Tennessee. The parish is not without problems, but within the congregation there are more than enough talents and resources for their solutions, with God's help.

EPISCOPAL CHURCHWOMEN OF ST. GEORGE'S EPISCOPAL CHURCH

Immediately after St. George's Mission was started, the women of the church and their friends organized a branch of the Ladies' Auxiliary and became active in all the work of the mission. Mrs. Joe A. Martin was president of the auxiliary. Other officers were Mrs. Gordon McCaa, vice-president; Mrs. Carl Graves, study leader; Mrs. Joe Kirby, United Thank Offering Custodian; Mrs. Mamie Cloyes, supply box president; Mrs. John B. Scruggs, social secretary; and Mrs. H. T. Adair, secretary and treasurer.[1]

One of their first acts was to furnish the proper colored hangings and linen for the altar and other furniture, which was placed on the lower floor of the Masonic Lodge Hall.

The Ladies' Auxiliary, along with the congregation and the church officers, began working to raise funds to build a chapel on the lot across the street. Through the generous response of individuals, other

---

[1] Pear Scruggs, "New Episcopal Mission at Germantown Now Completed," Unpublished, 1937. Appendix.

churches, and the Church Extension Fund of New York, they were soon successful.[2]

The altar linen for the new chapel was furnished by Mrs. Mamie Cloyes, whose mother in Austria sent it to her for that purpose.

On Wednesday, April 23, 1941, the Ladies' Auxiliary of St. George's Church gave a tea at "Mimosa," the home of Colonel and Mrs. James Hammond. The event honored the Reverend and Mrs. Charles L. Widney. More than two-hundred invitations were sent to Episcopalians to call at the Hammond home between four and six o'clock to meet the Reverend Mr. Widney, the new rector of St. George's, and Mrs. Widney. Receiving the guests with the Reverend and Mrs. Widney were Mrs. Hammond, Bishop and Mrs. James Maxon, Mrs. D. W. DeHaven, Mrs. Joe Kirby, Mrs. George Friedel, and Mrs. J. B. Hebron. The tea table, draped with a lace cloth and centered by an antique silver and crystal

---

[2] Louise F. Acklen, "Scrapbook of St. George's Episcopal Church" (1965), Unpublished. Appendix.

epergne, was presided over by Mrs. Carl Graves and Mrs. H. T. Adair. Spring flowers in pastel tones from the "Mimosa" gardens adorned the reception rooms.[3]

In 1950 the women held three fund-raising events for the purpose of buying stained glass windows for the church. Mrs. Frank King was president of the auxiliary. The first event was a card party and fashion show held at the Everett Cook home. The women also sold chances for a drawing for a fur stole. Mrs. Phoebe Cook, the mother of Mrs. Dunbar Abston, won the stole. The final event was a luncheon and card party at the Hunt and Polo Club on Cherry Road. The three events raised approximately $2000.00[4]

---

[3] The Commercial Appeal, April 19, 1941.
[4] Conversation with Helen O'Brien.

ST. GEORGE'S ANTIQUES ARCADE

In February of 1972 Mrs. Eric Catmur (Margaret) donated certain pieces of antique furniture from her home to be sold at auction under the auspices of church and/or church-school sponsorship for the express purpose of raising funds. The vestry of St. George's unanimously approved the idea, and the Women of the Church began working on plans in the spring of 1972.[5]

They decided to invite ten antiques dealers from the tri-state area to display and sell their antiques at St. George's along with the parish booth containing Mrs. Catmur's furniture.

The first Antiques Arcade was held October 26-28, 1972, and featured a French theme with a model of the Eiffel Tower in the center of the gymnasium. Mrs. Joseph E. Woodward (Eleanor) was chairman of the event, which produced approximately $3,000.00. The proceeds were divided between the Church Home and the Organ Fund.

---

[5] Vestry Minutes, May, 1972.

In 1973 Mr. Richard Simmons again created a masterpiece by building a replica of London's Big Ben for the center of the gymnasium. The clock weighed three-hundred pounds and was created from fifteen woods. The 1973 Antiques Arcade featured a little London Park for its decorations. The Big Ben clock is now located in the Germantown Village Square Mall. Eleanor Woodward was once again chairman of the arcade.

The 1974 Antiques Arcade under the chairmanship of Mrs. Jack McDonald (Sis) and Mrs. M. T. Gates (Ann) featured a Holland theme. Mr. Richard Simmons created an eighteen-foot windmill for the event. It was surrounded by hundreds of fresh tulips and mums. Antiques dealers from seven states exhibited at the event.

The 1975 Antiques Arcade had two new features. On Friday morning, Mrs. J. Patrick Roddy, III, from Knoxville lectured on "Landmark Homes in Tennessee." Sixteen exhibitors were featured in the show. Another new feature was the "new collector" tags placed on items of one-hundred dollars or less. A handmade quilt, made by some women in the church, was a door prize for the show. Mr. and Mrs. George Dando loaned a 1912 Studebaker, parked outside the door, and the show featured an "Outdoor Cafe" theme. Mrs. Dean Campbell (Jean) was chairman of the show.

The 1976 Antiques Arcade, under the chairmanship of Mrs. Calvin Warfield (Shirley), had a large sailboat, the USS St. George, in the center of the gymnasium. During the show a three-member panel of experts appraised small antiques for a five-dollar donation.

Three local artists donated original works to be used as door prizes for the 1977 Antiques Arcade. Mrs. George Hume (Jan) chaired the show, which featured a Victorian bandstand for the "As We Were" theme. A Book Booth was a new facet of the show, featuring new and old collectable books.

The 1978 arcade featured dealers from seven states exhibiting English and American furniture, oriental rugs, silver, paintings, prints, jewelry, and accessories. An antique fire engine was the center of the decorations. The proceeds from the 1977 and 1978 arcades bought a van for the Church Home. Mrs.

Stephen Maroda (Agnes) was chairman.

A "Music and Flowers" theme dominated the 1979 arcade, which opened with a festive Preview Party with hors d'oeuvres and musical entertainment. Betty James (Mrs. Joseph) was chairman. A music box, owned by the Church Home, was a centerpiece for the decorations. Plate lunches were sold each day at the arcade, which featured fourteen dealers from seven states.

The 1980 Antiques Arcade enlarged to include the Parish Hall and increased the number of dealers to nineteen. Mrs. Otto Lyons (Nadine) was chairman of the event, which featured two lecturers: Mrs. Allen Cooke (Dee) spoke on arranging silk flowers, and John Brown lectured on "How to Use Antiques in a Contemporary Environment."

Victorian Toys dominated the 1981 arcade, and an awning was bought to go across the drive from the gymnasium to the parish hall. Guitarists and a harpist entertained at the Preview Party. Mrs. Tim Key (Pam) was chairman of the arcade, which raised $10,000.00.

Mrs. John Rockett (Carol Ann) was chairman of the 1982 arcade, which had a Woodland Fantasies theme. An arcade cookbook was sold, featuring favorite recipes of the women of the church and recipes from the arcade luncheon. Mimi Dann donated a porcelain piece for a door prize. The show cleared $15,000.00.

The 1983 Antiques Arcade, chaired by Mrs. James Breazeale (Beth), featured a Harvest theme with pumpkins and straw. Sixteen dealers from eleven states participated. One half of the proceeds was divided between the Church Home and the Churches and Social Services Fund.[6]

---

[6] Antiques Arcade Scrapbooks, clippings, and yearly reports. The author is indebted to Carol Ann Rockett for the research and composition of this section of the Appendix.

Organists and Choir

One of the most interesting and dramatic developments that has taken place during the fifty years of St. George's existence has been exhibited by the organists and choirs. When the mission began in the Germantown Masonic Lodge Hall, there essentially was no choir and a reed pump (manual) organ was the only musical instrument.[1] At times the organist was dependent upon several children to aid her in pumping to produce continuity in the music.[2] This organ continued to be used after the congregation moved into the Chapel until the late 1930s when a communicant, William (Bill) Terry gave the mission an electronic reed organ.[3] This instrument served the congregation until 1954 and after the parish had relocated. In that year upon the recommendation of Dr. Thomas Webber,

---

[1] Interview with Elizabeth P. Hughes, January, 1984.
[2] Interview and notes of Ednamae Thompson, April, 1984.
[3] See note 54, The Mission Years, supra.

then the organist at Idlewild Presbyterian Church, a Conn electronic organ was purchased through the donations of communicants and friends.[4] This instrument served the parish well until 1972 when it became apparent it must be replaced. Throught the leadership of the rector and the organist a group within the parish, the "Organ Organizers" raised $30,000.00 for the purchase of a fifteen rank Reuter pipe organ which was installed in 1973. It was dedicated at an Evensong and Concert on October 7, 1973 with full choir.[5] This instrument was moved and installed in the new sanctuary in 1979.

As previously mentioned, when the mission began a choir did not exist. Even at the cornerstone laying service and the consecration service, the choirs of other churches performed.[6] There was only a small choir in the late 1940s and early 1950s in the Chapel

---

[4] Interview and note of Ednamae Thompson, April, 1984.
[5] Interview and note of Nancy Sutton, March, 1984.
[6] See notes 31, 39, The Mission Years, supra.

because of available space.[7] After the parish moved to the new location in 1954, duets and quartets were necessary since the choir still consisted of only six members. During this time a junior choir was formed under the direction of Elizabeth Anderson.[8]

There was no substantial growth in the parish's music program until 1969, several months after Nancy Hagemeyer (Sutton) became organist and choirmaster. In that year the adult choir had grown to eighteen members and the junior choir numbered twenty.[9] Also in that year the choir room on the second floor of the west end of the church building was enlarged.[10]

The choir continued to grow in quality and number and by 1980 the adult choir had forty members with twenty-five choristers in the junior choir.[11] As the

---

[7] Interview with Ednamae Thompson, April, 1984.
[8] Ibid.
[9] Interview and notes of Nancy Sutton, March 6, 1984.
[10] Ibid.
[11] Ibid.

parish moves into its fiftieth year, Mrs. Sutton is now a full time organist and choirmaster.

With the completion of the new church building in 1979 St. George's musical program took on a new dimension in quality. In 1982 the Association of Anglican Musicians, an international professional organization of organists and choirmasters, held its conference in Memphis. On the evening of June 24, 1982 the parish was honored to host an evening concert of baroque music with orchestra and the combined choirs of St. George's and Calvary churches conducted by Mrs. Sutton. Since that performance Mrs. Sutton and the choir have had three festal evensong concerts. On November 21, 1982, the Franz Schubert Mass in G; on March 27, 1983, an Evening with Johann Sebastian Bach, and on November 13, 1983, Antonio Vivaldi's Gloria were performed. All were not only well-attended by parishoners and friends in community, the concert on November 13, 1983 was performed to a capacity congregation.

St. George's Organists and Choirmasters

Elizabeth Powell	1934-1941
Hugh Smith	1941-1950
Ednamae Thompson	1950-1958
Helen Aiken	1958-1964
Leslie Casaday	1964-1966
Hugh Tones	1966-1968
Larry Ladd	2 months in 1968
Nancy Sutton	1968-1984

PRIESTS AND RECTORS OF ST. GEORGE'S
From Parish Register No. 1

	Began	Terminated
Charles F. Weller Archdeacon	June 14, 1934	
Dr. Sterling Tracy*		
Rev. David S. Rose**		
Rev. Thomas P. Simpson**		
Rev. Guy S. Usher	Jan. 1, 1940	Jan. 1, 1941
Charles Leonidas Widney	Mar. 1, 1941	April 22, 1952
Rev. Thomas A. Roberts	Aug. 31, 1952	Oct. 1, 1956
Frank Mauldin McClain	June 1, 1957	Aug. 15, 1962
David E. Babin	Sept. 1, 1962	Aug. 31, 1965
Robert Cherry	Sept. 1, 1965	Jan. 1, 1967
Sidney Ellis	April 1, 1967	Aug. 1, 1971
Chester Allen Cooke	Sept. 1, 1971	

* First Priest-in-Charge, began March, 1937
** Supply Clergy

ST. GEORGE'S EPISCOPAL MISSION AND PARISH VESTRY OFFICERS

Senior Wardens:

John B. Hebron	1934-1942
Carl R. Graves	1943
Charles Kortrecht	1944-1947, 1953
Turk Humphrey*	1948-1952 (In 1949 John Scruggs served from 14 Feb. to 14 March)
Dennis Dean	1954
Joseph Walden	1955 (Resigned September)
Dunbar Abston	1955 (From September)
Dennis Dean	1956-1957, 1961-1962 Resigned
James O'Brien	1958, 1962 (2 mos.), 1967
Eric Catmur	1959-1960
Walter Wills	1963
Steve Bledsoe	1964
Frank King, Jr.	1965
William Cowan	1966
George Jones	1968
Lee Winchester	1969
Louis Vance	1970

* Vestry Minutes reflect John Scruggs was elected in 1949 but Diocesan Parochial Reports show Turk Humphrey. John Scruggs resigned on 14 March 1949.

Senior Wardens, Continued

Richard Douglas	1971
Elton Turnipseed	1972
Jack McDonald, Jr.	1973
Wayne Neibel	1974
M. "Rusty" Gates	1975
Dean Campbell	1976
Thomas Young	1977
Calvin Warfield	1978-1979
Leonard V. Hughes, Jr.	1980
Jean Campbell	1981
James Breazeale	1982
Clark Doan	1983
George Hume	1984

Junior Wardens:

Carl Graves	1935-1942
None	1943
Dunbar Abston	1944
Frank King	1945-1946
Dunbar Abston	1947
Ed Dillard	1948

Junior Wardens, Continued

Turk Humphrey**	1949
Dennis Dean	1950-1951
Vance Alexander	1952
Pembroke Pinkney	1953
Hiram Adair	1954
Hiram Adair	1955
James O'Brien	1956-1957, 1960, 1962
Walter Wills	1958-1959
Kenneth Robertson	1961
George Jones	1963
Frank King	1964
Wise Jones	1965
Henry Mitchell	1966
Dan Allen	1967-1968
William Douglas	1969
Bob Black	1970
Elton Turnipseed	1971
Richard Douglas	1972
Horace Nelson	1973

** Vestry Minutes reflect Turk Humphrey elected in 1949, but Diocesan Parochial Report shows Dennis Dean.

Junior Wardens, Continued

Henry Witte	1974
Mrs. Jack "Sis" McDonald	1975
Thomas Young	1976
George Hume	1977
Gene Young	1978
William Dugard	1979
Richard Cowan	1980-1981
Otto Lyons	1982
Dean Campbell	1983
Dean Campbell	1984

Treasurers:

Charles E. Speers	1934
John B. Scruggs	1935-1937
W. C. Robertson	1938-1941
Margaret L. Finley	1942
S. E. Rison	1943
Ed Dillard	1944-1946
Kenneth Robertson	1947-1960, 1962
Henry Mitchell, III	1961
Bayliss Lee	1963
John Acklen	1964-1969
Loucas S. Dimou	1970-1984

Vestry Clerks:

Joseph A. Martin	1934-1936
No record	1937
Alfred Holden	1938
No record	1939
John Scruggs	1940-1943
William L. Lawler	1944-1945
Kenneth Robertson	1946-1948
James O'Brien	1949-1952
Frank King, Jr.	1953
E. T. McHenry	1954-1956
Alexander Dann	1957-1958
John Haizlip	1959-1960
Otto Lyons	1961
Louis Ochs, Jr.	1962-1963 - 3/25/63
Wise Jones	1963 - 5/27/63
R. Boyd Pickens	1965-1966
William Russell	6/13/66 - 1967
Elden Dye	1968
Fred Husbands	1969
George Hume	1970
Knox Everson	1971
Leigh Ferguson	1972

Vestry Clerks, Continued

Eleanor Woodward	1973-1975
Ann Moffatt	1976 - 3/8/76
Jan St. Andrew	1976
Evelyn Lagenbach	1977
Dean Campbell	1978-1979
William Dugard	1980-1981
William Bettison	1982-1983
John Killian	1984

CHURCH SCHOOL SUPERINTENDENTS

1934 -	Carl R. Graves	1958 -	Phillip P. McCall
1935 -	Carl R. Graves	1959 -	Phillip P. McCall
1936 -	Carl L. Graves	1960 -	John Haizlip
1937 -	Mrs. Otto Lyons	1961 -	John Haizlip
1938 -	Mrs. Otto Lyons	1962 -	Dr. George P. Jones, Jr.
1939 -	Mrs. Otto Lyons	1963 -	Dr. George P. Jones, Jr.
1940 -	Mrs. Otto Lyons	1964 -	Mrs. Lee Winchester & Mrs. Dan Allen
1941 -	Mrs. Otto Lyons	1965 -	Mrs. Lee Winchester
1942 -	Rev. C. L. Widney	1966 -	Mrs. Steve Bledsoe
1943 -	Rev. C. L. Widney	1967 -	W. Wise S. Jones & R. H. Lee Winchester, Jr.
1944 -	Rev. C. L. Widney		
1945 -	Rev. C. L. Widney	1968 -	John M. Glenn
1946 -	Mrs. Otto Lyons	1969 -	John M. Glenn
1947 -	Mrs. Otto Lyons	1970 -	L. Hall Jones, Jr.
1948 -	Mrs. Otto Lyons	1971 -	Horace W. Nelson
1949 -	Mrs. Otto Lyons	1972 -	D. Wayne Neibel
1950 -	Mrs. Otto Lyons	1973 -	D. Wayne Neibel
1951 -	Mrs. Otto Lyons	1974 -	Hulon Warlick
1952 -	Mrs. Otto Lyons	1975 -	Robert Vernon
1953 -	J. T. Jones	1976 -	Gabe E. Allen
1954 -	W. Joe Moore	1977 -	Gabe E. Allen
1955 -	W. Joe Moore	1978 -	James Thorell
1956 -	W. Joe Moore	1979 -	James Thorell
1957 -	W. Joe Moore	1980 -	Edward Carman
		1981 -	Jock Tooley, Chairman, Ch. Ed. Comm.
		1982 -	Jock Tooley, Chairman, Ch. Ed. Comm.
		1983 -	Carol Ann Rockett, Chairman, Ch. Ed. Comm.
		1984 -	Carol Ann Rockett, Chairman, Ch. Ed. Comm.

LICENSED LAYREADERS AND CHALICEBEARERS
FROM DIOCESAN JOURNALS

1934 - 1948 -	John B. Scruggs
1949 -	Jere L. Crook, John B. Scruggs
1950 -	None listed
1951 -	J. T. Jones, Jr.
1952 -	William Joe Moore
1953 -	William Joe Moore
1954 -	William Joe Moore, J. T. Jones, Jr.
1955 -	William Joe Moore, J. T. Jones, Jr.
1956 -	William Joe Moore, J. W. O'Brien
1957 -	William Joe Moore
1958 -	Eric A. Catmur, Otto F. Lyons, Jr., Thomas S. Young, III
1959 -	James W. O'Brien, Otto F. Lyons, Jr., Eric A. Catmur, Thomas S. Young, III, William C. Cowan, John Haizlip, Alex W. Dann
1960 -	Alex W. Dann, Jr., Thomas S. Young, III
1961 -	John Haizlip, Alex W. Dann, Jr., Thomas S. Young, III, James T. Jones, Jr., James W. O'Brien, Otto Lyons, Jr., Eric Catmur
1962 -	None listed
1963 -	None listed
1964 -	Edward C. Boldt
1965 -	Edward C. Boldt, Ernest McAfee
1966 -	Edward C. Boldt, Ernest McAfee, Otto F. Lyons, Jr., Charles F. Hinricks
1967 -	Edward C. Boldt, Otto F. Lyons, Jr., Ernest W. McAfee, Jr., Charles F. Hinricks, Alex W. Dann, James W. O'Brien
1968 -	Edward C. Boldt*, Charles F. Hinricks, Otto F. Lyons, Jr., Ernest W. McAfee, Jr., H. Charles Doan, Elton Turnipseed
	*Also licensed Chalice Bearer, 1968 Canon 49, Sec. 5
1969 -	Otto Lyons, Jr.*, Charles F. Hinrichs, Ernest W. McAfee, Elton G. Turnipseed, Jr.
	*Also licensed Chalice Bearer, 1969 Canon 49, Sec. 5
1970 -	Otto F. Lyons, Jr., Ernest W. McAfee, Jr.*, Elton Turnipseed
	*Also licensed Chalice Bearer, 1970, Canon 49, Sec. 5
1971 -	Otto F. Lyons, Jr. Ernest W. McAfee, Jr., Elton Turnipseed*
	*Also licensed Chalice Bearer, 1971, Canon 49, Sec. 5
1972 -	Milbourne T. Gates, Otto F. Lyons, Jr.*, Elton G. Turnipseed*
	*Also licensed Chalice Bearer, 1972 Title III, Canon 25, Sec. 5

LICENSED LAYREADERS AND CHALICEBEARERS
FROM DIOCESAN JOURNALS

1973 - Milbourne T. Gates*, Otto F. Lyons, Jr.*, Elton Turnipseed, Jr.
*Also licensed Chalice Bearer, 1973, Title III, Canon 25, Sec. 5

1974 - M. T. Gates*, Otto F. Lyons, Jr.*, Elton G. Turnipseed, Jr.*, James W. O'Brien, Charles E. Stuart, Thomas S. Young, III
*Also licensed Chalice Bearer, 1974, Title III, Canon 25, Sec. 5

1975 - Ronald Bence, M. T. Gates*, Otto F. Lyons, Jr.*, James W. O'Brien, Charles E. Stuart, Elton G. Turnipseed, Jr.*, Thomas S. Young, III
*Also licensed Chalice Bearers, 1975, Title III, Canon 25, Sec. 5

1976 - Ronald Bence, M. T. Gates*, Otto F. Lyons, Jr.*, James W. O'Brien, Charles E. Stuart, Elton G. Turnipseed, Jr.*, Thomas S. Young, III
*Also licensed Chalice Bearers, 1976, Title III, Canon 25, Sec. 5

1977 - Ronald Bence, William T. Dugard, M. T. Gates*, Otto F. Lyons, Jr.*, John McCarroll, Jr., James W. O'Brien, Charles E. Stuart, Elton G. Turnipseed, Jr.*, Thomas S. Young, III
*Also licensed Chalice Bearers, 1977, Title III, Canon 25, Sec. 5

1978 - James W. O'Brien, William T. Dugard, M. T. Gates*, Otto F. Lyons, Jr.*, John McCarroll, Jr., James Parnell, Charles E. Stuart, Elton G. Turnipseed, Jr.*, Thomas S. Young, III
*Also licensed Chalice Bearers, 1978, Title III, Canon 25, Sec. 5

1979 - H. Dean Campbell, Eric Catmur, Jim Creamer, H. Clark Doan, William T. Dugard, M. T. Gates*, Otto F. Lyons, Jr.*, John McCarroll, Jr., James W. O'Brien, James E. Parnell*, Germaine Peterson, James D. Russell, Elton G. Turnipseed, Jr.*, Thomas S. Young, III
*Also licensed Chalice Bearers, 1979, Title III, Canon 25, Sec. 5

1980 - Howard Dean Campbell*, Eric Alan Catmur, Henry Clark Doan, William Thomas Dugard*, Milbourne Thornton Gates*, Otto Franklin Lyons*, John Ramsey McCarroll, Jr.*, James Walter O'Brien*, James Eugene Parnell*, Germaine Dominques Peterson, James Dennis Russell, Elton Gilbert Turnipseed, Jr.*, Gerald Paul Yates, Thomas Sloan Young, III
*Also licensed Chalice Bearers, 1980, Title III, Canan 26, Sec. 5

LICENSED LAYREADERS AND CHALICEBEARERS
FROM DIOCESAN JOURNALS

1981 - H. Dean Campbell*, Eric A. Catmur, Clark Doan,
William T. Dugard*, Milbourne Thornton Gates*,
Otto F. Lyons, Jr.*, John McCarroll, Jr.*, James
W. O'Brien*, Germaine Peterson, Jim Russell,
Elton G. Turnipseed, Jr.*, Gerald Yates, Thomas
S. Young, III*
*Also licensed Chalice Bearers, 1981, Title III,
Canon 26, Sec. 5

1982 - H. Dean Campbell*, Clark Doan*, William T. Dugard*,
Milbourne Thornton Gates*, Otto F. Lyons*, John
McCarroll, Jr.*, Germaine Peterson*, Jim Russell*,
Gerald Yates*, Thomas S. Young, III*
*Also licensed Chalice Bearers, 1982, Title III,
Canon 26, Sec. 5

1983 - H. Dean Campbell*, Eric A. Catmur, Clark Doan*,
William T. Dugard*, M. T. Gates*, Otto F. Lyons,
Jr.*, John McCarroll, Jr.*, Germaine Peterson*,
James Russell*, Gerald Yates*, Thomas S. Young,
III*, Mary Lynn Wenzler
*Also licensed Chalice Bearers, 1983, Title III,
Canon 26, Sec. 5

1984 - The Diocese of West Tennessee
H. Dean Campbell*
H. Clark Doan*
William T. Dugard*
Milbourne Thornton Gates*
Otto Lyons, Jr.*
John R. McCarroll, Jr.*
James D. Russell*
Gerald Yates*
Thomas Young*
Millard Fillmore Bowen, IV
G. Gregory Meeks
Mary Lynn Wenzler
*Also licensed Chalice Bearers, 1984, Title III,
Canon 26, Sec. 5

GROWTH OF ST. GEORGE'S MISSION AND PARISH THROUGH THE YEARS
(From Parochial Reports, Diocesan Archives)

Year	Number of Communicants	Total Budget, Operating and Capital Expenditures
1934	17	131.43
1935	15	296.88
1936	26	316.15
1937	21	332.50
1938	24	444.68
1939	25	707.12
1940	46	1,506.76
1941	90	1,461.90
1942	110	2,276.60
1943	98	3,101.84
1944*	108	3,058.51
1945	109	**11,119.50
1946	116	**15,104.15
1947	130	5,276.22
1948	128	5,808.64
1949	135	5,514.90
1950	137	5,268.95
1951	140	7,237.71
1952	100	**16,255.16
1953	123	**12,377.20
1954	135	**13,881.45
1955	159	**14,484.33
1956	173	25,089.39
1957	169	22,840.00
1958	185	27,726.04
1959	195	25,598.43
1960	203	28,670.38
1961	247	29,061.95
1962	252	37,148.67
1963	231	**56,438.62
1964	261	42,711.32
1965	279	44,059.10

*Parish status achieved.
**Includes building funds.

Year	Number of Communicants	Total Budget, Operating and Capital Expenditures
1966	341	41,067.87
1967	403	51,496.68
1968	437	**63,534.87
1969	468	59,320.68
1970	478	63,759.55
1971	475	74,350.38
1972	485	103,634.26
1973	479	123,538.45
1974	473	105,244.77
1975	511	**119,712.00
1976	558	**128,971.00
1977	623	**149,147.00
1978	641	**665,867.00
1979	639	**331,410.00
1980	707	265,278.00
1981	632	225,271.00
1982	708	260,333.00
1983	780	299,189.00

** Includes building funds.

Sources and Bibliography

Almost every church historian suffers from a dearth or absence of early church records. This has been the situation, to some extent, with the early records and materials of St. George's Mission. Fortunately, Pearl Scruggs saw the need to document the formation and early activities of the mission. She left for us two chronicles, one she titled "New Episcopal Mission at Germantown Now Completed" which appears to have been written prospectively as a news release. The article appearing in the Commercial Appeal on March 29, 1937 regarding the Chapel consecration closely conforms to Mrs. Scruggs' language. Her second chronicle titled "History of the Mission in Germantown, Tennessee" consists of only a page and one-half typewritten compared to three typewritten pages for her first chronicle. Both of these have been duplicated as Documents 6 and 8 respectively in the Appendix. A third chronicle which was also probably written by Mrs. Scruggs is duplicated as Document 7, however, it is attributed to John Scruggs because it was included in his scrapbook and differs slightly from the other two documents. Strangely enough, it cites the correct date for the consecration but gives an incorrect date for the cornerstone laying service. It now seems clear that Document 6 is a corrected copy of Document 7 even though the correction on the date of consecration was in error.

One of the primary sources at the author's disposal was parish registers. The first register has been an invaluable source of information, but it is also clear that many or probably most of the entries were not made until sometime in 1940, six years after the mission was organized. An analysis of Register 1 indicates that at the time the entries of communicants were made one of the founders, Joseph Martin, was deceased. He died on December 28, 1939. The first baptism entered was that of Denise Phillips and her brother, Stewart, the date of which originally was not entered. Since coincidentally the first baptism became the author's wife, the date of that baptism actually occurred on September 22, 1940. The remaining baptisms are not chronological, but entered nunc pro tunc. The marriages are chronological and begin on December 15, 1940. There is one group entered on the confirmations dated November 14, 1937, but the confirmation of two persons on March 28, 1937 is absent. See note 39, The Mission Years, supra.

For the period which this history attempts to cover definitively vestry minutes existed for only six years, that is, from 1949 to 1954. It therefore was necessary to rely on oral sources, Diocesan Journals and records, newspaper articles and collateral sources which were given to the author by interested friends of the parish. Most of the photographs presented in the text as well as Documents 1, 7, 9, 11, and 17 represent the latter.

Special recognition is accorded to Mr. Kenneth Robertson who assisted the author in the research, collection of materials in addition to providing his personal knowledge of the congregation since 1934. The author also recognizes and thanks those who provided assistance by oral interviews or correspondence on the following page titled Oral Sources.

ORAL SOURCES

INTERVIEWS

Kenneth Robertson,
Germantown, Tennessee

Carl R. Graves,
Destin, Florida

Mrs. Thomas Roberts (1982),
Greenville, South Carolina

Elizabeth Speer McGhee,
Memphis, Tennessee

Elizabeth Anderson,
Germantown, Tennessee

Mrs. W. E. Cheairs,
Memphis, Tennessee

Mrs. Betsy West,
Memphis, Tennessee

Mrs. John Stivers,
Germantown, Tennessee

Barbara Apperson,
Germantown, Tennessee

Nanie Mae Holden,
Memphis, Tennessee

Ramona Graves,
Memphis, Tennessee

Jane K. Williamson,
Memphis, Tennessee

James W. O'Brien (1982),
Germantown, Tennessee

Otto Lyons, Jr.,
Germantown, Tennessee

Dorothy Kirby Wills,
Memphis, Tennessee

Frances Robertson,
Memphis, Tennessee

James T. Jones,
Memphis, Tennessee

Thomas L. Phillips,
Memphis, Tennessee

Mrs. B. P. Mueller,
Collierville, Tennessee

Louise F. Acklen Rosengarten,
Memphis, Tennessee

Isabelle Scruggs Wade,
Memphis, Tennessee

Nora Holden Kellerhals,
Memphis, Tennessee

Theresa Williamson Bledsoe,
Bartlett, Tennessee

Betty McCall,
Germantown, Tennessee

ORAL SOURCES

INTERVIEWS

Ednamae Thompson,
Germantown, Tennessee

Mary Eva Lyons (1982),
Germantown, Tennessee

Harry F. Cloyes,
Germantown, Tennessee

Mrs. Hiram (Lotta) Adair,
Gulfstream, Florida

Robert (Bobby) C. Lanier,
Germantown, Tennessee

Virginia C. Phillips,
Memphis, Tennessee

Mrs. Clarence Smith,
Germantown, Tennessee

Mrs. Morgan Zook,
Gulfstream, Florida

Anne Pickering,
Germantown, Tennessee

Elizabeth Baker Parr,
Collierville, Tennessee

A. B. Chambers,
Memphis, Tennessee

Mrs. Josephine Roberts Spruill,
Columbia, South Carolina

The Reverend Canon George Fox,
Memphis, Tennessee

Mrs. Gaither Hatcher,
Memphis, Tennessee

Dorothy Robertson
Memphis, Tennessee

Helen O'Brien
Germantown, Tennessee

Mrs. Charles Kortrecht
Memphis, Tennessee

Linton Weeks,
Tybee Island, Georgia

The Reverend Guy S. Usher,
Dallas, Texas

Judge Carl Graves
Destin, Florida

The Reverend Joe Moore
Cordova, Tennessee

Mrs. Eric Catmur
Memphis, Tennessee

ORAL SOURCES

INTERVIEWS

Virginia McDonough (Winston),
Dallas, Texas

Nancy Sutton,
Germantown, Tennessee

The Reverend Sidney Ellis,
Panama City, Florida

The Reverend Frank M. McClain
Winnetka, Illinois

Joan Cowan
Forest Hill, Tennessee

APPENDIX
HISTORICAL DOCUMENTS
INDEX

Document   1. Letter from Bishop Frank Gailor to Dr.
                 E.T. Yancey, October 5, 1893.

Document   2. Report of the Chancellor of the Diocese
                 of Tennessee, January 18, 1923.

Document   3. Report of Committee to the Bishop Co-
                 Adjutor, January 15, 1924.

Document   4. Application to the Bishop for the
                 organization of Mission, August 1, 1934.

Document   5. Card for solicitation of donations
                 1935, 1936.

Document   6. New Episcopal Mission at Germantown
                 Now Completed by Pearl Scruggs, 1937.

Document   7. New Episcopal Mission at Germantown
                 Now Completed, John B. Scruggs,
                 August 9, 1938.

Document   8. History of the Mission in Germantown,
                 Tennessee, by Pearl Scruggs.

Document   9. Letter from Charles Knight Weller to
                 John B. Scruggs, August 9, 1938.

Document   10. Articles of Association of St. George's
                 Parish, Germantown, Tennessee,
                 January 30, 1944.

Document   11. Letter from Charles Knight Weller to
                 Pearl and John Scruggs, April 10, 1944.

Document   12. Floor Plan, New Building, 1953-1954.

Document   13. Notes by Mrs. Dennis Dean, May 16, 1962.

Document   14.   Scrapbook of: The History of St.
                  George's Episcopal Church of Germantown,
                  Shelby County, Tennessee by Margaret
                  Louise Finley Acklen, 1965.

Document   15.   History Note - 1970.

Document   16.   Newspaper photograph and article, later
                  added to scrapbook, 1966.

Document   17.   Letter from Vestry to Communicants,
                  November 21, 1955.

DOCUMENT 1

Sewanee Tenn.
Oct. 5- 1893.

Doctor E.T. Yancey,
Germantown, Tenn.

My dear Sir:

I shall be in the neighborhood of Germantown about Dec. 6th & shall be glad to visit Germantown & hold service there on Dec. 7th - if you will kindly arrange for it -

Very sincerely yrs,
Thos. F. Gailor
Asst Bishop of Tennessee

DOCUMENT 2

Gentlemen of the Convention:-

The will of W. W. Bott of record in the office of the Clerk of the Probate Court of Shelby County, Tennessee, in Will Book 17, pages 266, contains the following provision:-

> "My lot in Germantown - part of it - one acre I give for Church lot to the Episcopal Church and in fond remembrance of the Rev. John Blount, deceased, of the Lillieshall Parish Church, Salop, England."

Acting under this provision and reciting its terms, Charles M. Haynie and J. J. Miller, Executors of W.W. Bott, conveyed to the Convention of the Protestant Episcopal Church in the Diocese of Tennessee, a lot described as follows:-

> " One acre of land, being part of the real estate owned by W. W. Bott, deceased, in Germantown, beginning at the southeast corner of the lot conveyed by the grantors herein to Matilda A. Garner, running thence South sixty-two and one half (62 1/2) degrees East eighteen and one half (18 1/2) links; thence east one hundred and sixty-three (163) links; thence north eight (8) degrees east one hundred and forty-five and one half (145 1/2) links; thence north sixty-six (66) degrees east four hundred and thirty links; thence north forty-seven (47) degrees West one hundred and thirty-one (131) links; thence south eighty-eight (88) degrees West one hundred and twenty-three (123) links; thence south two (2) degrees West one hundred and thirty (130) links; thence south sixty-six (66) degrees West one hundred and six and seven hundredths (106 7/100) links; thence south sixty-four (64) degrees west one hundred and seventy-seven and fifty-seven hundredths (177 57/100) links; thence south eight degrees West two hundred and forty-two and four tenths (242 4/10) links to the beginning."

This deed is dated March 27, 1905, and is recorded in the office of the Register of Shelby County, Tennessee, in Book 364, page 454.

I have been unable to ascertain how the boundaries as set forth in the deed were defined, but in any event the Convention is the owner of the property described.

A proposition has been made by the Strickland heirs to exchange for the lot above described a lot owned by them in Germantown, described as follows:-

> "Beginning at the intersection of the east line of Spring Street with the north line of the first public road south of the Southern Railway; thence east with such North line seventy (70) feet more or less to the west line of the Presbyterian Church lot; thence north with said west line one

hundred and seven and forty-eight hundredths
hundredths (107.48) feet; thence west fifty-
nine and five tenths (59.5/10) feet to the east
line of Spring Street; thence south with such East
line one hundred and seven and nine tenths (107-9/10)
feet more or less to the point of beginning."

The lot conveyed to the Convention by the Executors of Bott is unsuited for Church purposes. It is rough, low and uneven and is on the line of the Southern Railway. The lot offered in exchange by the Strickland heirs, while not as large as the lot now owned by the Convention, is admirably suited for Church purposes. It is high, level and well located. I advise the acceptance of the proposition as made, but would suggest the appointment of a committee of three to fully investigate the situation and the entry on the minutes of an order authorizing the execution of the deed necessary to complete the transfer, should the Committee thus appointed approve the plan. The contemplated order should be substantially as follows:-

> The Convention having considered the report of the Chancellor relative to the exchange of the lot now owned in Germantown for other property owned by the Strickland heirs (both lots being fully described in the report, it was ordered:-
>
> That _____, and _____, be and are hereby appointed a Committee to investigate and report to the Bishop on the advisability of the proposed exchange, and should such report be in favor thereof the Bishop is hereby authorized to execute such deeds as may be necessary to effect the transfer. The execution of such conveyance by the Bishop shall be considered as conclusive evidence of his right to do so under the provisions of this resolution, and no subsequent purchaser shall be required to examine or consider such report as the Committee may make."

No matters of legal importance have been brought to my attention during the past year that would adversely affect the Diocese.

Respectfully submitted.

_____
Chancellor.

DOCUMENT 3

To the Rt. Rev. James M. Maxon, Bishop Co-Adjutor:

At a meeting of the 91st annual convention of the Protestant Episcopal Church in the Diocese of Tennessee, held on January 17th and 18th, 1923, the following resolution was adopted:-

> Resolved: That the Convention, having considered the report of the Chancellor relative to the exchange of the lot now owned in Germantown for other property owned by the Strickland heirs, both lots being fully described in the report: Mr. W. Poston Maury, Dr. E.T. Yancey and the Chancellor of the Diocese be and are hereby appointed a Committee to investigate and report to the Bishop on the advisability of the proposed exchange; and should such report be in favor thereof, the Bishop is hereby authorized to execute such deeds as may be necessary to effect the transfer. The execution of such conveyance by the Bishop shall be considered as conclusive evidence of his right to do so under the provisions of this resolution, and no subsequent purchaser shall be required to examine or consider such report as the above named Committee may make.

After carefully considering the situation your Committee is of opinion that the exchange of property referred to in the report of the Chancellor should be made, **provided** the title to the property offered to the Convention by the Strickland heirs is good.

We are largely influenced in this decision by the fact that we have found it impossible to identify the property conveyed to the Convention by Chas. M. Haney and J.J. Miller, Executors of W. M. Bott, though we have had frequent conferences with surveyors and frequent consultations with each other. Since it seems to be impossible to identify the property which we now own, we deem it advisable to exchange such title as we may have for the lot referred to offered us by the Strickland heirs.

Jany 15 1924

E. T. Yancey
W. Poston Maury.

DOCUMENT 4

APPENDIX F
APPLICATIONS TO THE BISHOP
FOR ORGANIZATION OF MISSIONS

I. ST. GEORGE'S MISSION, GERMANTOWN

Germantown, Tennessee, August 1, 1934.

Right Reverend Father in God:—

We the undersigned, residents of Germantown, and its environment, in the County of Shelby, Diocese of Tennessee, being desirous of obtaining the services of the Church, and ready, according to our several ability, to sustain the same, do hereby request you to provide for us as you may deem proper and expedient. We do hereby declare ourselves, individually and collectively, ready to do whatever may be necessary to establish and sustain the regular worship of the Church. We do hereby promise conformity to the doctrine, discipline, liturgy, rites and usages of the Episcopal Church; and further, we promise to obey the Constitutions and Canons of the General Convention and of the Diocese of Tennessee. We, therefore, hereby ask to be organized as a Mission under the name of St. George's Mission. Furthermore, we do hereby specially stipulate and agree to raise annually toward the support of our stated Minister the sum of one hundred and twenty ($120.) dollars, and at least twenty-five ($25.) dollars annually toward the support of the Diocese, and at least the sum of thirty-five ($35.) dollars toward the support of the Church's Program, known as the Apportionment, these to be paid in monthly instalments.

Remaining obediently yours in the Church,

(Signed) John Bell Hebron, Mary Hebron Graves, Carl R. Graves, John B. Scruggs, Mrs. Mamie Cloyes, Chas. E. Speer, Elizabeth D. Speer, Mrs. H. T. Adair, Edwin S. Williamson, J. A. Martin, Francis Martin, Geraldine Apperson Martin.

DOCUMENT 5

WILL you please help to make our little congregation happy by contributing one dollar, or any amount you choose, to complete this little chapel?

Saint George's Mission
GERMANTOWN, TENN.

DOCUMENT 6

NEW EPISCOPAL MISSION AT GERMANTOWN
NOW COMPLETED

Dedication and Consecration Services will be Conducted by Bishop Maxon Easter Sunday

1937 March 17

St. George's Episcopal Mission at Germantown, the corner stone of which was laid October 4th, 1936, has now been completed and will be dedicated and consecrated at 4 P.M., Easter Sunday, March 28, 17th, 1937.

The Very Reverend James M. Maxon, Bishop of the Diocese of Tennessee, assisted by a number of the Memphis Episcopal clergy, will conduct the services. The quartet of St. John's Episcopal Church will assist with the music.

Fifty years ago a Mr. Botts of Olive Branch, Miss., gave a lot at Germantown to the Diocese of Tennessee. During this long period of time the few communicants in the neighborhood have attended the Episcopal churches in Memphis and at Collierville, and somehow never got around to building a church at Germantown, and the building site was almost forgotten.

In 1933 John B. Scruggs of Germantown was made lay reader in St. Andrew's Church at Collierville. The Venerable Charles K. Weller, now retired, then archdeacon of West Tennessee, was rector. In recent years the number of communicants in the Germantown neighborhood has increased considerably, but their attendance at Collierville and Memphis was irregular on account of the distance.

Doctor Weller called the attention of Mr. Scruggs to the lot at Germantown, and suggested that now was an opportune time to build a mission there, and offered his assistance and influence.

A meeting of all the communicants in the neighborhood was called June 17, 1934, and St. George's Mission was organized. The vestry was composed of J. B. Hebron, Senior Warden; Joe A. Martin, Secretary;

John B. Scruggs, Treasurer and lay reader; Carl Graves, Junior Warden and superintendent of the Sunday School. An auxiliary was organized, composed of Mrs. Joe A. Martin, President; Mrs. Gordon McCaa, Vice-President; Mrs. Carl Graves, study leader; Mrs. Joe Kirby, United Thank Offering Custodian; Mrs. Mayme Cloyes, Supply Box President; Mrs. John B. Scruggs, Social Service Secretary, and Mrs. H. T. Adair, Secretary and Treasurer.

Arrangements were made to conduct services regularly in the Eastern Star rooms of the Masonic Lodge, and then began the task of raising the money to build the chapel.

Cards were printed and sent out to many Episcopal Church communicants in Tennessee, and the generous response with contributions was very gratifying. Several communicants in the neighborhood contributed substantial sums, and a large portion of the sum necessary for building the chapel was furnished by the Church Extension Fund of New York, a body of the Episcopal Church.

The efficiency of the U. S. Engineers was indirectly responsible for one large donation. A man in Germantown who owns a large plantation in Mississippi along "Old Man River," and who had already contributed handsomely to the building fund, promised the finance committee that if the levees held the recent flood off his plantation he would make an additional contribution of a hundred dollars. The levees withstood the strain, and he made good his promise.

The construction of the building, and the grading and beautifying of the lot was superintended by H. T. Adair with the assistance of J. B. Hebron, Senior Warden. The actual work was done by Finley.

A handsome brass cross for the altar was given by Grace Church of Memphis, and the baptismal font was given by Church of the Good Shepherd. The hardware on the doors was contributed by Mrs. Ben Henderson of Memphis. The litany desk and lecton which have been in use in the temporary quarters, and which were made in accordance with standard specifications, have been refinished and given to the new chapel by John D. Scruggs. The cross on the exterior of the church is a duplicate of the St. George crosses used in England. Ivy from historic Westminster Abbey in London will eventually adorn the new chapel. was in London a few years ago, and obtained permission to take a few cuttings of the famous ivy. These cuttings were transplanted in Memphis, and cuttings from that will be transplanted at St. George's Mission.

The altar linen is from Austria, and was furnished by Mrs. Mayme Cloyse, whose mother in Austria sent it to her for that express purpose.

The silver communion service, which Germantown communicants have used for forty years, and which has been in the possession of Mrs. Ben Bruce of Germantown, was given by her to the new chapel.

The interior of the chapel is somewhat different in design from that of any other Episcopal church in West Tennessee. The walls are covered entirely with figured ply-wood which shows up to beautiful advantage after being finished with cherry shellac. The chapel is gas heated and electrically lighted. The lamps resemble old time kerosene lamps, and hang in clusters of three.

The leafy arms of a giant oak spread protectingly over the sanctuary of the little chapel, and lend picturesqueness to the setting.

NEW EPISCOPAL MISSION AT GERMANTOWN
NOW COMPLETED

Dedication and Consecration Services will be Conducted by Bishop Maxon Easter Sunday

St. George's Episcopal Mission at Germantown, the corner stone of which was laid October 6, 1935, has now been completed and will be dedicated and consecrated at 4 p.m., Easter Sunday, March 28.

The very reverend James M. Maxon, Bishop of the Diocese of Tennessee, assisted by a number of the Memphis Episcopal clergy, will conduct the services. The quartet of St. John's Episcopal Church will assist with the music.

Fifty years ago a Mr. Botts of Olive Branch, Miss., gave a lot at Germantown to the Diocese of Tennessee. During this long period of time the few communicants in the neighborhood have attended the Episcopal churches in Memphis and at Collierville, and somehow never got around to building a church at Germantown, and the building site was almost forgotten.

In 1933 John B. Scruggs of Germantown was made lay reader in St. Andrew's Church at Collierville. The Venerable Charles K. Weller, now retired, then archdeacon of West Tennessee, was rector. In recent years the number of communicants in the Germantown neighborhood increased considerably, but their attendance at Collierville and Memphis was irregular on account of the distance.

Doctor Weller called the attention of Mr. Scruggs to the lot at Germantown, and suggested that now was an opportune time to build a mission there, and offered his assistance and influence.

A meeting of all the communicants in the neighborhood was called June 17, 1934, and St. George's Mission was organized. The vestry was composed of J. B. Hehren, Senior Warden; Joe A. Martin, Secretary; John B. Scruggs, Treasurer and lay reader; Carl Graves, Junior Warden and Superintendent of the Sunday School. An auxiliary was organized, composed of Mrs. Joe A. Martin, President; Mrs. Gordon McCan, Vice-President; Mrs. Carl Graves, study leader; Mrs. Joe Kirby, United Thank Offering Custodian; Mrs. Mayne Cloyes, Supply Box President; Mrs. John B. Scruggs, Social Service Secretary, and Mrs. H. T. Adair, Secretary and Treasurer.

Arrangements were made to conduct services regularly in the Eastern Star rooms of the Masonic Lodge, and then began the task of raising the money to build the chapel.

Cards were printed and sent out to many Episcopal Church communicants in Tennessee, and the generous response with contributions was very gratifying. Several communicants in the neighborhood contributed substantial sums, and a large portion of the sum necessary for building the chapel was furnished by the Church Extension Fund of New York, a body of the Episcopal Church.

NEW EPISCOPAL MISSION AT GERMANTOWN
COMPLETED

New Episcopal Mission at Germantown completed.-

The efficiency of the U. S. Engineers was indirectly responsible for one large donation. A man in Germantown who owns a large plantation in Mississippi along "Old Man River", and who had already contributed handsomely to the building fund, promised the finance committee that if the levees held the recent flood off his plantation he would make an additional contribution of a hundred dollars. The levees withstood the strain, and he made good his promise.

The construction of the building, and the grading and beautifying of the lot was superintended by H. T. Adair with the assistance of J. E. Hebron, Senior Warden. The actual work was done by Finley.

A handsome brass cross for the altar was given by Grace Church of Memphis, and the baptismal font was given by Church of the Good Shepherd. The hardware on the doors was contributed by Mrs. Ben Henderson of Memphis. The litany desk and lectern which have been in use in the temporary quarters, and which were made in accordance with standard specifications, have been refinished and given to the new chapel by John S. Scruggs. The cross on the exterior of the church is a duplicate of the St. George crosses used in England. Ivy from historic Westminster Abbey in London will eventually adorn the new chapel.

_____ was in London a few years ago, andobtained permission to take a few cuttings of the famous ivy. These cuttings were transplanted in Memphis, and cuttings from that will be transplanted at St. George's Mission.

The altar linen is from Austria, and was furnished by Mrs. Mayme Cloyse, whose mother in Austria sent it to her for that express purpose.

The silver communion service, which Germantown communicants have used for forty years, and which has been in the possession of Mrs. Ben Bruce of Germantown, was given by her to the new chapel.

The interior of the chapel is somewhat different in design from that of any other Episcopal church in West Tennessee. The walls are covered entirely with figured ply-wood which shows up to beautiful advantage after being finished with cherry shellac. The chapel is gas heated and electrically lighted. The lamps resemble old time kerosene lamps, and hang in clusters of three.

The leafy arms of a giant oak spread protectingly over the sanctuary of the little chapel, and lend picturesqueness to the setting.

DOCUMENT 8

Mrs Johnston

History of the Mission in Germantown Tenn.

About the first of June 1934, at the request of several members of the Church living in or near Germantown The Archdeacon of West Tennessee, Rev. Charles K. Weller met with these Church people in the home of Mr. Joseph A. Martin, Forest Hill, where he explained the proper proceedure in the formation of a Mission according to the Canons of the Diocese. An application to the Bishop and Council was prepared, and the same was signed by the following, Mr. J. B. Hebron, Mr. & Mrs. Joseph A. Martin, Mrs. Mamie Cloyce, Mrs. J. B. Kirby, Mr. & Mrs. Hiram T. Adair, Mr. & Mrs. Carl R. Graves, and Mr. John B. Scruggs, This application was sent to the Rt. Rev. James M. Maxon, D.D. the Bishop Co-Adjutor, under whose care the Missions of the Diocese was given by Bishop Thos. F. Gailor. the Diocesan at that time. Bishop Maxon accepted the application, under the name of St. Georges' Mission, and upon the nomination of the Archdeacon appointed the following officers to hold office until January 1st, 1935,: Mr. J. B. Hebron, Warden, Mr. Joseph A. Martin, Secretary and Treasurer, Mr. John B. Scruggs, Layreader, these, with Messrs Carl R. Graves and Hiram T. Adair to compose the "Bishop's Committee of the Mission.

Mr. Scruggs became active at once, and secured the use of the lower floor of the Masonic Building for services every Sunday until such time as we could erect our own chapel, his activities included the securing of an Altar, Prayer Desk, Lecturn and Altar Rail, for our first service which was held Sunday morning June 17th, 1934 at 11.00 A.M. by the Archdeacon, The ladies of the Mission became active and shortly furnished the proper colored hangings and linen for the Altar, and other furniture, Services were continued every Sunday with Mr. Scruggs as Layreader, except the third Sundays when the Archdeacon held the Holy Communion and preached. Many extra services were held by Bishop Gailor and the Clergy of

Memphis from time to time.

The congregation at once began the accumulation of funds for the erection of a Chapel, and on October 11th, 1936 the Archdeacon laid the Corner Stone, he was assisted by the Rev. W. T. Dakin of the Diocese of Mississippi and Mr. John B. Scruggs, the choir of St. Johns' Church Memphis kindly furnishing the music.

The building was completely finished and furnished without debt early in 1937, and consecrated by Bishop Maxon on March 17th, 1937. The Archdeacon, who had retired on January 1st, was not able to be present, but visited the congregation the last Sunday in October and celebrated the Sacrament of Holy Communion and preached to a large congregation of his old friends and the new members.

Since his Ordination, the pastoral care of the Mission has been under the Rev. Dr. Sterling Tracy.

Immediately after the Mission was started the women of the Church and their friends organized a branch of the Woman's Auxilliary and have been active in all the work of the Mission

DOCUMENT 9

Bluff Springs Florida
August 9th, 1938

My dear John:

Your letter of the 3rd, inst. received, and I am enclosing a history of St. Georges' Mission as best I can remember, I trust that it is what you need. I was vary glad to hear from you again, and that Pearl is alright, give her our love.

I guess considering our age, both Mrs. Weller and I are getting along o'k, however last spring I was seriously ill with the flu and then a relapse, lost 45# in weight in six weeks, and it looked like I was nearing the end, however the Master seemed to have something more in life for me, and I now have regained my weight but not my strength, I am not as active as I once was, and tire easily, but I do go int o Pensacola each week to see the children, George and Nelson and their families, and on the first Sunday in the month assist with the Holy Communion at Christ Church, I am supplying all the services there this month while the rector is on his vacation, it is somewhat tiresome this ot weather, but I really enjoy being back in full harness for a while, I do miss it very much.

I have been very sad this past week on account of the death of two very close friends, the Rev. M. L. Tate, who has corresponded with me ever since I came here, in fact he wrote me a fine letter just before he died, and the other one was Mr. Benj Neely of College Park Georgia, the first man I presented for Confirmation and while that has been a long time ago, we have kept up a continual correspondence all these years. Mr. Tate was a year older than I, and Mr. Neely two year younger, I will miss them both, until the time comes when we will be re-united in that better World.

Mrs. Weller has her usual heart trouble occasionally, in fact before I finished the "History" here at my desk, she had one, and of course I am continually worried for fear that Dr. Lyle Motley's prophetcy comes true," a sudden end at any time", though she seems, except for that in better health and stronger than for years.

As to the reansfers at the starting of a Mission or Parish, the Church Law, as I remember it is, that those who sign the application become members, and that the Minister should so notify the rector or Minister in whose parish he or she had belonged, I so notified each rector in Memphis, and Mr. Bratton was the only one who acknowledged my notification with a transfer of the Martin Family. BUT if there is any question, all that your Minister has to do, is to request a transfer, and the Rector HAS TO GIVE IT if the member is NOW WILLING

I am looking forward to my possibly going to the Consecration of Dr. Dandridge on September 20th, in Nashville, if I do I will go with the Rev. Mr. Hodgkins of Pensacola who used to be the rector of the Church in Columbia Tenn. I will not know until he returns from his vacation trip.

Give my best regards to all my friends in Germantown.

Sincerely

DOCUMENT 10
ARTICLES OF ASSOCIATION

of ST. GEORGE'S PARISH   GERMANTOWN, TENNESSEE

Whereas, the following named persons, Communicants of the Protestant Episcopal Church, resident in Germantown, Tennessee, and vicinity, in Tennessee, viz:

Mrs.Jos.B.Kirby,Mrs.D.W.Dean,Mrs.Frank King, Mrs.L.D.May,Mrs.John B.Scruggs, Mrs.Anne May Webb,Mrs.Carl R.Graves,Mrs.Mamie Clayes,Mrs.Dunbar Abston, Mrs.Ben B.Henderson, Carl R.Graves, T.F.King, Dunbar Abston,Chas.H.Kortrecht, William H.Lawler,L.D.May,John B.Scruggs,Wm.J.Brown,Mrs.S.E.Rison,W.P.Mitchell with others, have associated together for the purpose of organizing a Parish according to the Doctrine, Discipline, and Worship of the Protestant Episcopal Church in the Diocese of Tennessee, they do hereby declare the following to be the articles and conditions of their association:

(1). The title of this Parish shall be the Rector, Wardens and Vestrymen of St. George's Parish, Germantown, Tennessee.

(2). The Parish acknowledges and accedes to the Constitution, Cannons, Doctrine, Discipline and Worship of the Protestant Episcopal Church in the Diocese of Tennessee.

(3). The affairs of this Parish shall be conducted by the Vestry, consisting of the Rector, Wardens and Vestrymen thereof, according to the Constitution and Canons of the Church. The Rector, when present, shall preside ex-officio at the meetings of the Vestry.

(4). The Rector of this Parish shall be elected by the Wardens and Vestrymen in open meeting, duly convened for that purpose.

(5). The Wardens and Vestrymen of this Parish shall all be registered Communicants of the same.

(6). The Parish, or any Trustees in whose name the property of the Parish shall be vested, shall not by deed or by any other means, without consent of the Bishop, under his hand, or (in case of a vacancy in the Episcopate) of the Standing Committee of this Diocese by a major number thereof, under their hands, previously had and obtained, grant, alien, or otherwise dispose of any lands, messuages, tenements, or hereditaments in them vested for the use and benefit of said Parish, nor charge nor encumber the same to any person whomsoever.

(7). All real estate shall vest in the Convention of the Protestant Episcopal Church in the Diocese of Tennessee, in trust for this Parish.

[signatures]

Proposed Budget for Self-Support

Stipend of Minister	1800.00	
House Rent	360.00	
Total Stipend & House Rent	2160.00	2160.00
Pension Fund Assessment, 7.5 % of $2160.00		162.00
Diocesan Assessment		52.00
Running Expense (Without Organist or Car allowance)		326.00
Total		$2700.00

Easter Offering for Church Program $120.00

"Articles of Association"
of
St. George's Parish
Germantown
1944

Admitted 1/30/44

BALLON, GRAVES & NICHOLSON
ATTORNEYS AT LAW
PORTER BUILDING
MEMPHIS, TENN.

DOCUMENT 11

THE VEN. CHARLES KNIGHT WELLER
RETIRED ARCHDEACON, DIOCESE OF TENNESSEE
900 SOUTH SECOND STREET
POST OFFICE BOX 4734, WARRINGTON
PENSACOLA, FLORIDA

April 10th, 1944

My dear Pearl & John:

   It was quite a pleasure to receive your good letter of March 30th, I was very sorry to learn of your mothers passing away, and of John's illness, of course your mother had lived a good long life, and if you study the teaching of the Easter message in the Gospel of yesterday, you can rejoice that the time will come when you will see her in her happiness in the presence of the Master, for that is what life is for, and as you pass the "three score and ten" years, you feel the nearness of that reunion.

   I always feel a special interest in the Church in Germantown, and when thinking of it, I feel that without the influence of John B. Scruggs there will not/any St. Georges Church there. I of course feel that the Blessed Master led us together, and He used me to assist John in that good work, as John grows older that little church will mean more and more to him, he has my love and prayers always, and his good wife deserves lots of credit for standing by him.

   For my age, I am in good health, of course I get tired more easily, but carry on trying to keep up my little home here, with a fine garden and many roses and other flowers and chickens to care for. God was very kind to me in giving me a good companion in my old age, of course she has a hard time following the Angel that was my helpmeet for 46 years, but she does her best to make me happy.

   I still keep going in the Church work, went to Panama City (108 miles away) for both the services yesterday, and perhaps it was just to make me feel good, but the young deacon, who is just out of the Seminary at Sewannee told me after the service that my sermon was the best he had ever heard, and that I had put much feeling in delivering it. the subject was "the hope of the Resurrection" from the text "I am He that liveth, and was dead, and behold I am alive forevermore."

   I hope sometime to return to my old friends in Tennessee, but of course we must wait for the end of the war. My son Heber is a Major, and chaplain in the Pacific, Nelson is in the Navy and located at Key West, his family are with him, My son George and Heber's family live near me here in Warrington which makes me quite happy.

   Give my love to my friends that you meet,

          Affectionately
          Chas. K. Weller

DOCUMENT 12

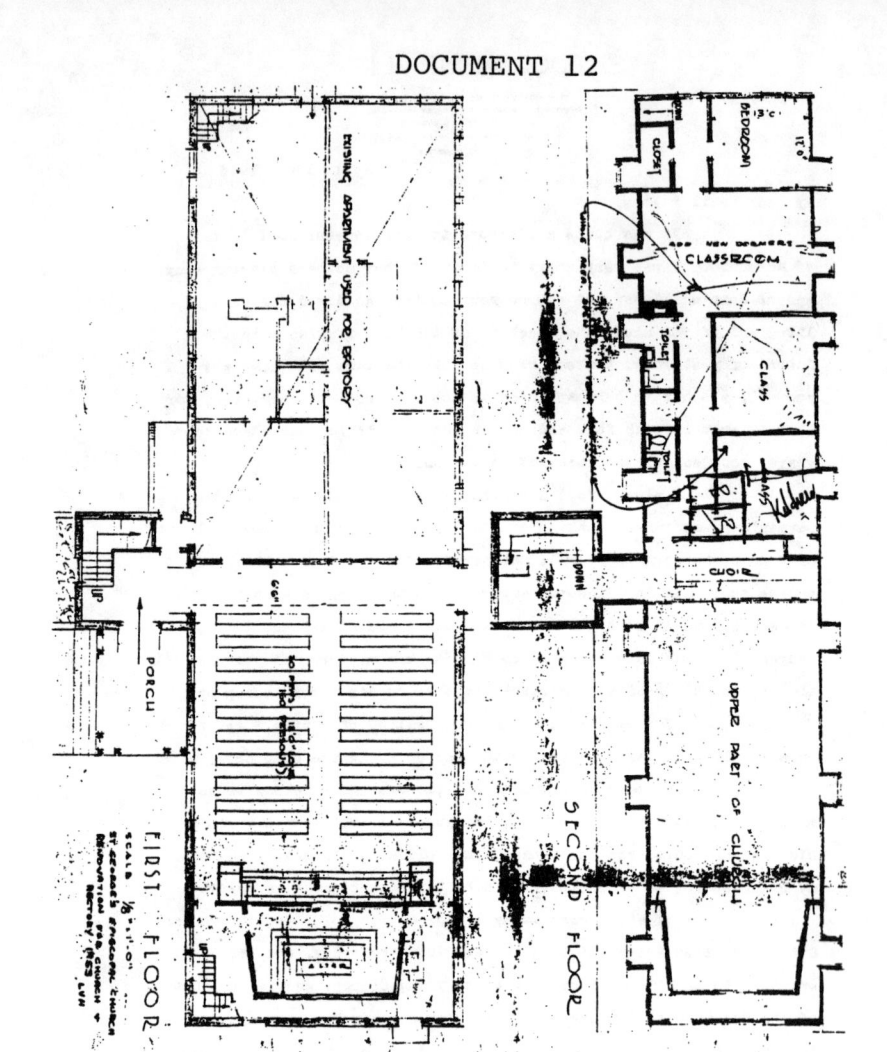

DOCUMENT 13

1.

5-16-62

To bring you up to date on our numerical and financial position, I will use the Parochial Report of December 31st, 1956 (being the last annual record prior to Mr. McClain becoming our rector) and, by way of comparison, the December 31st, 1961 Parochial Report covering his last full year as rector of St. George's.

May I state here inadequate records available in 1956 have been brought up to date and are current. No reflection is intended on Mr. Roberts for whom we all have the highest regard but, without the services of a secretary, and because of sadly neglected previous records, Mr. Roberts was unable to maintain needed records. However, due to the painstaking and time-consuming efforts of Mr. McClain and the aid of our assistant secretary, our records are now accurate and up to date.

On Dec. 31, 1956 we showed the number of baptized persons in our parish as 263. However, keep in mind that this figure included some of who had died and many who had moved away and their whereabouts were unknown. As of Dec. 31st, 1961 the number of active baptized persons in the parish had increased to 353.

The number of families in 1956 was shown on the records as 65. However this number was shortly reduced by 9 families by eliminating those who had moved away or were inactive. Our last report in 1961 showed 81 active families - a gain of 25 families plus 49 individuals (not classed as families) and 10 inactive (residing out of the area).

In 1956 there were 9 baptisms, against 13 in 1961; and confirmations rose from 15 in 1956 to 29 in 1961. Our overall active communicants for 1961 increased to 243 against 173 in 1956.

Comparing the number of services held in 1956 and 1961 - other than Holy Communion, there were 121 in 1956 against 120 in 1961. (You will note 1 less regular service in 1961, but there was a very large increase in the services of Holy Communion- from 108 in 1956 to 246 in 1961 - more than twice as many).

And now I will give you the figures of which we are most proud - the increase in our Church School. At the end of 1956 our Church School consisted of 9 teachers and about 75 children under 18 years of age, but by the end of 1957, under less than six months of Mr. McClain's guidance, the teachers had increased to 15 (a 66-2/3% increase) with very little increase in the number of children. By the end of 1961 children under 18 years of age had increased to 132, but with only 2 additional teachers since 1957. We are very proud of the increase in pupils but are sorry that teachers only increased by 2, or a 13% increase in teachers against a pupil increase of 76%.

May I digress from this report at this time to say that it would be impossible to teach our church school pupils, the majority of whom are 12 years of age or under, without our present educational building. Prior to the new building, I have seen classes being taught in the narthex, out on the grounds and in the hallway of the parish house. Some of you who attend the 7:30 or 11 o'clock services can hardly visualize an average Sunday attendance of 114 during November, 1961 at the 9:30 service. Our Church School has, more than once last year, gone over 150 for a Sunday service so I want to add that this building was needed and in the planning stage long before there was any thought of a Day School. However we are happy that we now have our Day School making use of this building during the week since the building is for the purpose of serving this parish in its Christian educational work and for any other activity that will further the Church's efforts in this parish. Notwithstanding the long and urgent need for this building, I am sorry to have to report that only the small number of 49 of our parishioners out of a total of 130 potential contributors made a pledge or contributed to this project. But for the financial help of some friends outside our parish family, it might still be in the planning stage, instead of furnishing us this meeting room we are enjoying tonight, and affording us the classrooms to instruct our youth. May I add here, we still have need of considerable funds to equip and furnish this building and we are in a receptive mood for any contributions or pledges which may be paid over the next three years in any way you care to handle it.

Having touched on the financial needs of the building fund, I now come to our General financial condition and needs. For that I shall again compare the budget for 1957 with the budget for 1962, having you keep in mind the numerical increase and that our activities have about doubled. In 1956 our total attendance at all services was 8,005 whereas, in 1961, our total attendance was 12,761, an increase that any rector can point to with justifiable pride. May I suggest that you show your appreciation to Mr. McClain for the splendid results he has accomplished.

These results were accomplished on a total operating expenditure in 1961 of $27,669.67 against $21,432.00 in 1956 and, in 1956 we had the expense of a priest for only nine months. Our parish has almost doubled numerically, the services have more than doubled and our operating costs have only increased about 32%.

In comparing the budget for 1957 of $21,774. with the proposed budget for 1962 of $29,337., we find an increase of only 37%. Of this increase $5,791.20 covers items over which we have no control- viz. apportionment, assessment and Quintard House, all three items being fixed equitably for all churches by the Diocese. Back in 1957 these three items were only $4,113. Our proposed budget for 1962 is only $2,517.40 over last year and the only increase is in those items over which we have no control. Our vestry carefully considered each item and reduced operating costs on other items by $900 below the 1961 budget.

Our mortgage debt on the educational building is $60,000. increasing our operating cost in interest, utilities and insurance premiums. For the time being the building fund pledges are being used to retire the principal debt with the interest charge being included in the general fund budget as an operating expense. So, the erection of our educational building increased our opportunities for Christian service to the parish and community, but it likewise increased our operating costs- Interest, utilities and insurance premiums increased our expense approximately $640 monthly, part of which will be met out of building fund pledges as they mature and are paid.

Finally I come to that part of this report which is most discouraging. Out of 128 envelopes mailed out only 79 have made a pledge giving us a total of $23,203, falling short $6,134.80 of meeting our budget. I feel sure that a prospective rector is going to be most interested in how we meet this deficit and will feel somewhat skeptical of accepting a call to a church showing at the outset its inability to meet its financial needs.

We certainly must make every effort to complete the every member canvass at once and plans will be made to this end as well as to give our new parishioners an opportunity to share in the financial needs of the church. I trust that those parishioners who have overlooked or failed for any reason to complete their pledge will do so at once.

The Calling Committee and its function
Vestry issues call
Conclusion - Work for every parishioner. We have been too complacent waiting for "George" to do it.

Budget - 1961 - $26,820.40
" - 1962 - 29,337.80
Pledged - " 23,203.00
short 6,134.80

DOCUMENT 14

Scrapbook of:

THE HISTORY OF ST. GEORGE'S EPISCOPAL CHURCH of

Germantown, Shelby County, Tennessee.

Compiled by:

Margaret Louise Finley Acklen .
    (Mrs. John S.)

Dedicated to the Glory of God in memory of:

The Messers.:   John B. Scruggs
                J. B. Hebron
                Joe B. Kirby
                Mark Roy Finley.

INDEX

Page 1. History of St. George's Episcopal Church.

5A. Newspaper clippings - Laying of corner stone and
5B. commemorating services of the beginning of construction
5C. of St. George's chapel building.

5D. Photo of St. George's Altar as it looked in fall of 1937; Newspaper clipping of story of first confirmation service.

5E. Photo of inside of St. Georges chapel as it looked just after completion.

8. Old Church Bulletins.

9. Newspaper clipping of Blessing of St. Hubert.

10. Newspaper clipping of news of by gone days - 25 yrs. ago.

11. Order of Services for the Ordination to the Priesthood of our rector, Thomas A. Roberts.

12. Newspaper clipping of the story of Rev. Thomas A. Roberts.

13. Newspaper story and photo of purchase of Winston property.

14. Newspaper clipping of proposed plans for remodeling of recently purchased property.

15. Newspaper clipping- Wedding announcement of our rector, Rev. Frank Mauldin McClain to Miss Mary Lee McGinnis.

16. Newspaper clipping- Rev. & Mrs. McClain cutting wedding cake.

17. Newspaper clipping of St. George's Church Day School.

18. Newspaper clipping- ground breaking for school.

19. Newspaper clipping- school dedication services.

20. Newspaper clipping- Evensong services.

21. Newspaper Clipping of story of Rev. David E. Babin.

22. Newspaper clipping- wedding announcement of Maxine Mitchel.

23. Newspaper clipping- God & Country award to scout.

24. Newspaper clipping- Tree planting at school.

25. History of the Germantown Community Episcopal Churches.

26. Church officials - beginning with original Bishop's Committee.

FOREWORD.

The idea of the history of St. George's Episcopal Church of Germantown, Tennessee, being compiled in book form and of such a book being called the "GREAT BOOK" was originated several years ago by the Reverend Frank Mauldin McClain who was rector of St. George's at the time. Members of the congregation were asked to bring any pictures, newspaper clippings, etc., that might be used to the church office.

The later part of 1963 I was told the materials were still in the church office; and, little realizing just what I was volunteering for, I volunteered to carry out the original plans of a book on the history of St. George's. After a year of compiling the few available materials, gathering some data by making personal visits, telephone calls, gathering some information from a history of Germantown, written by Mr. A. H. Holden, and being faced with the fact that much of the very necessary data needed in writing a church history was lost due to the fact that St. George's had no office for so many years, plus the fact that I am definitely not a writer, I've decided that it is best that this be in the form of a scrapbook rather than attempting to carry out the original idea of the "GREAT BOOK". However, I do feel that the information contained herein is of interest;and,if it is kept and added to in the future, perhaps someday the "GREAT BOOK" may be written by someone who has the ability to write it.

My sincere thanks go to each and everyone who has helped me to obtain the information contained herein.

Louise F. Acklen
(Mrs. John S.)

THE HISTORY OF ST. GEORGE'S EPISCOPAL CHURCH
GERMANTOWN, TENNESSEE.

The later part of the 1800's a lot was given to the Diocese of Tennessee by a Mr. Botts of Olive Branch, Mississippi. This lot was located at the Northeast corner of Germantown Road and West Street and was to be used at such time as it was needed on which to erect a place of worship for the Episcopal communicants of the community. There being so few such communicants in the community at that time, the lot was accepted but went unused for the next fifty years or so. During this time the Episcopalians in the Germantown community attended churches in Memphis or Collierville at irregular intervals, due to the distances between these churches and Germantown and to the lack of public transportation and even to the scarcety of privately owned means of travel. However, during these years, Episcopalians often met in private homes for the purpose of worship.

Mr. John B. Scruggs of Germantown, Tennessee, was made layreader in St. Andrew's Church of Collierville, Tennessee, in 1933. The Venerable Mr. Charles K. Weller, Rector of St. Andrew's at that time, was also archdeacon of West Tennessee; thus, Mr. Scruggs was called upon to perform his duties as layreader at regular intervals. Being a very sincere man with great devotion for his Church and his fellow man and realizing the steady increase in the number of Episcopalian communicants in Germantown, Mr. Scruggs was becoming more and more deeply interested in establishing a mission in Germantown. Dr. Weller called Mr. Scruggs' attention to the unused and almost forgotten lot at Germantown and suggested now was an opportune time to begin plans for a mission in Germantown. He offered his assistance and influence toward the building of such a mission.

A meeting of all Episcopal communicants in the community was called to meet at the home of Mr. and Mrs. Joseph Martin in Forest Hill, Tennessee, about the first of June, 1934. The meeting was held at the request of and under the direction of the Reverend Mr. Charles W. Weller who explained the proper procedure in the formation of a mission according to the Canons of the Diocese. An application to the Bishop and the Council was prepared and signed by the following:

    Mr. J. B. Hebron

    Mr. & Mrs. Joseph A. Martin

    Mrs. Mamie Cloyes

    Mrs. Joe B. Kirby

    Mr. & Mrs. Hiram T. Adair

    Mr. & Mrs. Carl Graves

    Mr. John B. Scruggs

This application was sent to the Right Reverend James M. Maxon, D. D., the Bishop Co-Adjutor, under whose care the Missions of Tennessee were given by Bishop Thomas F. Gailor. Bishop Maxon accepted the application of archdeacon Weller and appointed the following gentlemen to office until January 1st, 1935:

    Mr. John B. Scruggs, Lay-reader

    Mr. J. B. Hebron, Warden

    Mr. Joseph A. Martin, Secretary

    Mr. Charles Speers, Treasurer

These gentlemen along with Messers.: Carl R. Graves and Hiram T. Adair were appointed to compose the "Bishop's Committee" of St. George's Mission.

Thus it might be said that St. George's Episcopal Church, Germantown, Tenn, came into existence about June 1st, 1934; however, I understand that meetings had been held in private homes, under the direction of Mr. Scruggs, prior to this date for the purpose of reading and studying the Bible.

The Bishop's Committee became active immediately upon their appointment and secured the lower floor of the Germantown Masonic building for its regular Sunday services until such time as a Chapel could be erected. An Altar, Prayer Desk, Lectern and an Altar Rail were secured before the first official service of St. George's Mission was held on Sunday, June 17th, 1934, at 11:00 A.M., by archdeacon Weller, assisted by Mr. John B. Scruggs, layreader.

The ladies were not sitting idly by during this time. They became active immediately and shortly furnished the proper color hangings and linens for the Altar and other furniture.

Services continued every Sunday with Mr. Scruggs presiding as layreader each Sunday except the 3rd Sunday of each month, when Archdeacon Charles K. Weller celebrated the Sacraments of Holy Communion and delivered the sermon. Many special services such as Baptisms, Christmas and Easter services were held by Bishop Maxon and visiting Memphis clergy from time to time during the next few years. During these years St. George's parish family was host to many visiting communicants from Memphis who seemed to truly enjoy their visits.

Immediately after the Mission was started the women of the Church and their friends organized a branch of the Women's Auxiliary and became active in all the work of the Mission.

The congregation and the officers at once began working toward raising funds to erect a Chapel on the lot at the Northeast corner of Germantown Road and West Street. Cards were printed and sent out to the various Episcopal Churches in Tennessee telling of the plans to build a Chapel for St. George's Episcopal Mission in Germantown. The generous response from individuals, other churches, and the Church Extention Fund of New York, a body of the Episcopal Church, was most gratifying. Even the efficiency of the U. S. Engineers, by whom Mr. Scruggs was employed, was indirectly responsible for one large donation. Mr. Joe B. Kirby, a resident of Germantown who owned a large Mississippi plantation along the banks of "Old Man River", and who had already contributed generously to the project, promised the finance committee that, if the levees held the flood waters of the then raging Mississippi River off of his plantation, he would make an additional contribution of one hundred dollars. The levees withstood the strain, the plantation was saved, and the finance committee received the hundred dollars.

Grading and beautification of the lot had begun earlier under the able direction of Mr. Hiram T. Adair, acting Superintendent, and Mr. J. B. Hebron, Sr. Warden. The corner stone was laid Oct. 11th, 1936, and actual construction was begun on the chapel of St. George's Mission. All construction was done by my father, Mark Roy Finley, contractor of Germantown, Tennessee, who hand finished the interior of the building as well as staining the windows and painting the outside of the building.

Archdeacon Charles K. Weller presided at the services commemorating the beginning of construction of the new building at 4:30 P.M., October 11th, 1936,

6.

Archdeacon Weller, was the last of a family of seven generations of Episcopal ministers, three of whom had served in Tennessee. His father, ordained in Atlanta, Georgia, in 1909, was formerly of the Episcopal Ministery of Memphis and his grandfather established the first Episcopal church in Nashville, Tennessee. The Saturday previous to the commemeration services at Germantown, Archdeacon Weller had announced his retirement, effective January 1st, 1937, and had expressed hopes that his presiding over those dedication services would terminate his official services to the Church. However, the building was not completed until the early part of 1937, and he was unable to attend those services but did visit the congregation the last Sunday in October and celebrated the Sacrament of Holy Communion and delivered the Communion sermon to a large congregation which included many of his old friends as well as many new members.

Official papers of the Church and the Diocese, a short history of the Mission, and a list of the approximately 100 people attending the services were deposited in the copper lined cornerstone. Among the the Memphis Clergy assisting in the servaces was the Reverend Mr. Dakin, a retired minister. Mr. John B. Scruggs, layreader of the Mission gave a short talk and the Gospel lesson was read by the Rev. Dankin. Music for the service was furnished by the choir of St. John's Episcopal Church of Memphis.

The building was completely finished and furnished without debt early in 1937. Dedication and consecration services were held at 4:00 P.M. on Easter Sunday, March 17, 1937, by Bishop Maxon who was assisted by a number of the Memphis Episcopal clergy. St. John's Episcopal Church of Memphis furnished a quartet to assist with the music.

DEDICATION SERVICES FOR MISSION PLANNED

Germantown Church Will Open With Easter Ceremony

BISHOP MAXON TO APPEAR

Ivy From Westminster And Austrian Linens Decorate Building—Work Began Last Fall

The leafy arms of a giant oak spreading protectingly over its sanctuary, with bits of ivy from historic Westminster Abbey and altar linen from Austria, St. George's Mission at Germantown will be dedicated Easter Day to the worship of God and as a memorial to the band of faithful communicants of the Episcopal faith responsible for its completion.

The Rt. Rev. James M. Maxon, Bishop of Tennessee, will officiate at the dedication and consecration of the latest church built by the Episcopal denomination in West Tennessee. The service will be at 4 o'clock tomorrow afternoon with clergy of Memphis churches and 14 members of Calvary Church choir under the direction of Adolph Steuterman assisting.

Dr. Tracy Is Named

Confirmation rites will be administered to candidates by Bishop Maxon. Dr. Sterling Tracy, ordained deacon on Jan. 17 at St. Mary's Cathedral by Bishop Maxon and assistant to the dean of the Convocation of West Tennessee, has been named deacon-in-charge of the mission.

Gifts from individuals and other churches have aided the communicants in completing the church for which the cornerstone was laid Oct. 11 at services conducted by the venerable Charles K. Weller, former archdeacon for West Tennessee.

The cross on the exterior of the building is a duplicate of the St. George Crosses used in England. The ivy transplanted on the grounds is from plants grown by Mrs. Ethel Calkins of Memphis from cuttings obtained by special permission from Westminster Abbey while on a visit to London.

Other Items Contributed

A brass cross for the altar was given by Grace Church and the baptismal font is the gift of the Church of the Good Shepherd. Hardware on the doors was contributed by Mrs. Ben Henderson of Memphis.

The litany desk, lecton and altar, which have been used in temporary quarters and which were made in accordance with standard specifications, have been refinished and given to the new chapel by John B. Scruggs. The altar linen was sent to Mrs Mayme Cloyes for the specific purpose for which it will be used by her mother an Austrian. A silver Communion service, which Germantown communicants have used for 40 years, and which has been in the possession of Mrs. Ben Bruce, was given by her to the chapel.

Differing in interior design from other Episcopal churches in this section of the state, the walls are covered with figured plywood finished with cherry shellac.

Chapel Gas Heated

The chapel is gas heated and electrically lighted, the lamps hanging in clusters of three and resembling the old kerosene lamps in design. H. T. Adair superintended the grading and beautifying of the lot with the assistance of J. S. Hebron, senior wardens and actual construction was by M. Finley of Germantown.

The completed building is a tribute to the faithful communicants of the Episcopal faith in Germantown who have labored untiringly to obtain a church in their midst. For almost 30 years, the little plot of ground at the intersection of two roads given to the Diocese of Tennessee by a Mr Botts of Olive Branch Miss., lay undisturbed while the few communicants in the neighborhood attended church in Memphis and Collierville.

Group Organized In 1926

In 1923, Mr Scruggs was made lay reader in St. Andrew's Church at Collierville, and his attention was called to the lot by Archdeacon Weller, who offered his assistance and influence in securing a building for worship services in the Germantown community. At a meeting of communicants on June 17, 1934, the mission was organized. The vestry was composed of J. S. Hebron, senior warden; Joe A. Martin, secretary; Mr. Scruggs, treasurer and lay reader; Carl Graves, junior warden and superintendent of the Sunday school.

The auxiliary was organized and composed of Mrs. Joe A. Martin, president; Mrs Gordon McCaa, vice president; Mrs Carl Graves, study leader; Mrs. Joe Kirby, United Thank Offering custodian; Mrs. Mayme Cloyes, supply box president, Mrs. John B Scruggs, social service secretary, and Mrs. H. T. Adair, secretary-treasurer.

Work Opened Last Fall

Arrangements were made to conduct services regularly in the Eastern Star rooms of the Masonic Lodge Building in Germantown. A generous response from communicants in the neighborhood, from churchmen of other denominations and a sum from the Church Extension Fund of New York and from persons from New York to California, enabled the members to start work last fall.

THE COMMERCIAL APPEAL

MEMPHIS, TENN., MONDAY MORNING, OCTOBER 12, 1936

Cornerstone Laid For St. George's Episcopal Mission At Germantown Service

The Rev. Charles K. Weller (left), archdeacon of West Tennessee, officiated yesterday at the St. George's Mission cornerstone services at Germantown in which the Rev. W. E Dakin (center), and John B. Scruggs, lay reader of the mission also participated.

Headed by the choir of St. John's Episcopal Church the procession moved across the lawn to the site of the new church services commemorating this beginning of erection of the building dedicated to their faith.

—Staff Photo by Day

5B

5D.

The Altar in St. George's Mission - Fall, 1937.

The gold colored candle sticks and matching vases were given by a
Miss Ramaige, in memory of her father, Rev. Ramaige, former rector
of Grace Church, Memphis, Shelby County, Tennessee.

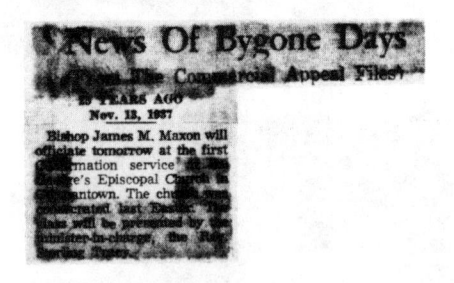

News Of Bygone Days
From The Commercial Appeal Files
15 YEARS AGO
Nov. 13, 1937
Bishop James M. Maxon will officiate tomorrow at the first confirmation service at St. George's Episcopal Church in Germantown. The church was consecrated last Easter...

Some present communicants of St. George's confirmed on this occasion included:
     Mrs. John B. Scruggs
     Miss Dorothy Kirby (Mrs. Walter D. Wills, Jr.)
     Miss Margaret Louise Finley (Mrs. John S. Acklen)

The hardware on the doors was contributed by Mrs. Ben Henderson. One approached the Chapel by a brick walk. The cross on the exterior of the chapel was a duplicate of the St. George crosses used in England. A giant oak tree, possibly over 50 years old, at the Northwest corner of the building spread its leafy arms protectingly over the sanctuary, thus lending a very picturesque setting to the white frame of the beautiful little chapel. This beautiful setting was further enhanced shortly by ivy from the historical Westminister Abbey of London, England. These cuttings were obtained by special permission a few years earlier and were transplanted in Memphis. Cuttings from these transplants were later planted at St. George's Mission in Germantown, Tennessee.

Grace Episcopal Church of Memphis gave a handsome Cross for the Altar and a beautiful Baptismal font. Gold candlesticks and matching vases were given by Miss _____ Ramaige, in memory of her father the Reverend Mr. _____ Ramaige, former Rector of Grace Episcopal Church of Memphis, Tennessee. A processional Cross and a Paten were given by the children in the Sunday Church School Mr. Bill Terry, Manager of the New York Giants Baseball Club, presented the new organ to the Mission. An American flag and stand were given by Mrs. Joe B. Kirby. The Litnay desk and the Lecturn, which had been built in accordance with standard specifications by the U. S. Engineers and had been used in the temporary quarters, had been refinished by Mr. Finley and were given to the new chapel by Mr. Scruggs. The Altar linens, hand woven in Austria, were given by Mrs. Mamie Cloyes, whose mother, Mrs. Albert vonArx, of Olten, Switzerland, had sent them to her for this express purpose. The silver Communion Service, in use by the Germantown Communicants for some forty years, and in the possession of Mrs. Ben Bruce of Germantown, was given by her. A beautiful round window, picturing the Virgin Mary holding the baby Jesus, was given by Mr. J. B. Hebron, in memory of his wife. Mr. Hebron's young grandson, Jack Graves, son of Mr. and Mrs. Carl Graves assisted his grandfather in selecting the window. This window was placed in the North wall of the chapel directly above the Altar. The Altar and Communion rail were built and hand finished by Mr. Finley.

The interior design of the chapel was somewhat different from that of any other Episcopal Church in West Tennessee. The walls were covered entirely with richly grained plywood which showed up beautifully after being hand finished with cherry shellac. The beautiful hand finished pews, of the early church pew design, were further enhanced by beautiful brass name plates, bearing the names of many prominent and active members. Heat was furnished from gas floor furnaces and it was lighted with very beautiful electric lights, resembling old time kerosene lamps, hung in clusters of three from the high ceilings with large wooden beams.

Shortly after his ordination, the pastoral care of the Mission was placed under the Rev. Sterling Tracy. His pastoral care of St. George's was succeeded by the Reverends: Guy S. Usher, Charles L. Widney, Thomas A. Roberts, Franm M. McClain, and David E. Babin, present Rector.

Directory of
St. George's Church

Wardens: J.N.Hebron, Carl Graves.

Treasurer: Carol Robertson

Clerk: John Scruggs (& Lay Reader)

Church School

Superintendent: Mrs. Otto Lyons

Secretary: Eva Marie Lyons

Teachers: Mrs.Carl Graves, Mrs. Thomas L. Phillips, Bettie Sue Hammond, W.G.Farr, Eva Marie Lyons.

Altar Guild

Directress: Mrs. Mamie Cloyce.

Auxiliary
(Meets Last Wednesday of Month)

President: Mrs. Geo.P.Friedel
Vice-President: Mrs W.G.Farr
Secretary: Mrs Carl Graves
Treasurer: Mrs. H.T.Adair
Devotional Secretary: Mrs.O.F.Lyons
Box Supply Sec.Mrs.Mamie Cloyce
United Thank Offering Custodian:
     Mrs. T.L.Phillips.
Social Service Sec:Mrs.John Scruggs.
Educational Sec. Mrs.Jeff Ward,Jr.

Choir
Mrs. Hugh Smith,Organist & Director

Young People's Service League
Sponsors: Mr & Mrs.T.L.Phillips.
President: William Farr.
V-President: Ebbin Rice.
Secretary: Barbara Friedel
Treasurer:Carl Graves, Jr.

Officers of Germantown Men's
Dinner Club: President:R.C.Burleigh
     Secretary: W.G.Farr

Katharine Adair, Sarah McCaa, Harry Lyons, received awards for four years perfect attendance at the Children's Lenten Services.

Is there anyone whose name you would like on the Herald's mailing list ?

Confirmation lectures for adults begin Tuesday, May 20, 7:45 p.m. Boys & Girls class Monday, May 19 , after school. Bring someone to confirmation.

The attendance at the preaching mission was very gratifying. We are also indebted to the clergy who preached each night.

The Easter offering was almost sixty dollars, over half the amount of our yearly quota to the Church Program.

If there are any mistakes or omissions in this bulletin, please forgive and let us have the corrections for future issues.

Have you placed your re-dedication card on the offering ? Let us go forward in service giving every talent that we have to God and His Church.

A PRAYER

O Lord Christ, against whose Church the gates of hell shall not prevail; grant to us in these days of storm and darkness the faith to trust in thee, and the courage to go forward in thy service; that we may be more than conquerors through thy power, who livest and reignest with the Father and the Holy Spirit, one God world without end. Amen.

Thursday, May 22, is Ascension Day
Holy Communion 10:30 a.m.

Would you like to give St. George's any of the following: An American Flag, The Episcopal Church Flag. Hymn board with slides of seasons.

ST. GEORGE'S HERALD

St. George's Episcopal Church
Germantown, Tennessee

Rev. Charles L. Widney
Telephone 40, Germantown

Bulletin: May 18, 1941

Page 2

We make our bow with bulletin one of St. George's Herald. If you know a better name, please tell us.

By action of the Vestry there will be no eleven o'clock service, May 25. We are giving way to the Commencement at the Germantown High School. Dr. F.B.Grear will preach the sermon.

There will be a baptismal service at 10:30 next Sunday, giving time for those attending the Commencement service to be at both.

The Auxiliary will meet Wednesday, May 28, 10 a.m. with Mrs. Hammond.

Next meeting of the Vestry is set for June 5, following the Men's supper.

Please keep your minister informed of those who are ill, or of newcomers.

Let's make St. George's Grow !

Page 3

The fine steps down to the street were constructed last week by Mr. Hebron and Mr. Robertson. They are of cypress, ought to last a long time, and will be convenient for those parking cars at the side of the Church.

Our thanks go to Mr. Sam Rison for the very complete mimeograph with which this bulletin is printed. It was a splendid gift to the Church and will be of great use to all of our organizations.

The Auxiliary has made possible the keeping of the Church open on stated days by arranging the closing off of the Vestry room. If you want to show St. George's to your friends some Sunday afternoon you will find it unlocked.

The card & pencil holders on your pew are the gift of Mrs. Graves.

Mr & Mrs J F Ward
Germantown Tenn

St. George's Episcopal Church
GERMANTOWN, TENNESSEE
The Rev. Charles L. Widney
Telephone 40

The Fall Kalendar
Please save for future reference.

September 28
    YOUTH SUNDAY. 11 a.m.
September 28 - October 5
    Religious Education Week
October 5
    FORWARD IN SERVICE SUNDAY
    Also, World Communion Sunday.
October 6 - 20
    Parish Program Conferences
October 28
    CONFIRMATION. 11 a.m.
    Bishop Dandridge.
November 9
    Presiding Bishop's Sunday. Nation
    Wide Broadcast. Columbia. 9 a.m. CST
    ANNUAL EVERY MEMBER CANVASS
November 11, ARMISTICE DAY.
    Church Wide Day of Prayer

Services
14th Sunday after Trinity
September 14, 1941
Daylight Saving Time.

7:30 a.m. Holy Communion

11 a.m. Morning Prayer & Sermon:
    "This Troubled World."

---

10 a.m. Church School

7 p.m. Young People's Service League.

Bishop Dandridge comes October 28 for confirmation. Class for Adults, Mondays, 7:45 p.m. at the Church.
Boys and Girls, Monday afternoons after school. At the Church.
Bring someone to Confirmation.

Directory of St. George's Episcopal Church
Germantown, Tennessee

Wardens: J. B. Hebron. Carl Graves.

Treasurer: Carroll Robertson

Clerk: John Scruggs (& Lay Reader)

EVERY MEMBER CANVASS
Chairman: J.B.Hebron.
Vice-Chairman: C.M.Kortrecht.

CHURCH SCHOOL

Superintendent: Mrs. Otto Lyons
Secretary: Eva Marie Lyons

Teachers: Mrs.Carl Graves, Mrs.Thomas L.Phillips, Mrs.Jep Ward,Jr. W.G.Farr, Barbara Friedel, Eva Marie Lyons, Joyce McCaa.

ALTAR GUILD

Directress: Mrs. Mamie Cloyce.

AUXILIARY
(Meets Last Wednesday of Month)

President: Mrs. Geo.P.Friedel
Vice-President: Mrs. W.G.Farr
Secretary: Mrs. Carl Graves
Treasurer:
Devotional Secretary: Mrs. O.F.Lyons.
Box Supply Secretary: Mrs. M.Cloyce.
United Thank Offering Custodian:
    Mrs. T.L.Phillips.
Social Service: Mrs. John Scruggs.
Educational Secretary: Mrs.J.F.Ward,Jr.

CHOIR
Mrs. Hugh Smith, Organist & Director.

Young People's Service League
Sponsors: Mr. & Mrs. T.L.Phillips.
President: William Farr.
Vice-President: Robin Rice.
Secretary: Barbara Friedel.
Treasurer: Carl Graves,Jr.

Officers of Germantown Men's Supper Club: President, R.C.Burleigh.
    Secretary, W.G.Farr

ST. GEORGE'S HERALD
Official Organ of St. George's Episcopal Church, Germantown, Tenn.

We are sure you will like the drawing of our beautiful church. It was done by Mr. J.F.Ward,Jr. We thank him for his gift to the bulletin.

Full schedule of services was resumed August 31. We are grateful to those who made our vacation possible. Your rector continued studies begun two years ago in the Sewanee Graduate School. Lecturer this summer was Dr. F.C.Grant, authority on the Old Testament.

Church School classes have started. New books for very interesting courses are on hand. Attendance is growing. Star pins will be awarded October 5 to pupils present four Sundays since September 1.

Rumors have it that we may expect a parish barbecue this fall. The ladies will decide at an Auxiliary meeting Wednesday, September 24th, at Mrs.O.F. Lyons. 10 a.m. Newcomers welcome !

Is there anyone whose name you would like on the Herald's mailing list ?

We regret so much losing Mr. & Mrs. Adair, Katharine and Nancy to Florida. We send the best wishes of St.George's.

Our good Presbyterian neighbors are having a Loyalty Church supper, Tuesday, Sept. 16, 6:30 p.m. 25 ¢ a plate.

The Vestry met last week and elected Mr. Hebron, chairman, and Mr.Kortrecht, vice-chairman, of the Annual Every Member Canvass. Date: Sunday, Nov. 9.

If there are any mistakes or omissions in this bulletin, please forgive and let us have the corrections for future issues of the Herald.

A new hymn board is promised soon. We still need a new American Flag, and a Church Flag. The organ is ours ! Final payment was made in July.

Oak Grove Hunt Given Blessing Of St. Hubert

Ancient Ritual is performed

By CATHERINE MEADE
Free-Scimitar Staff Writer

Reminiscent of the Frankish Middle Ages, when the ritual of St. Hubert, patron saint of the hunt, was invoked, the ceremony of the blessing of the hounds of the Oak Grove Hunt Club and a Thanksgiving service this morning at St. George's Church, Germantown...

...was held by the grooms...

...ally this centuries-old...
...called the "blessing...
...and the protect...
...hydrophobia.
...was asked as a ho[und?]...
...centuries in the...
...to the beauty of...
...the church was...
...by Rev. Jan Struther,
...Widney...
...river."
...hymn begins with th[e]
...Thee, Lord,
...Oak Thee, Lord,
...and gallant ho[unds]
...in pastures...
...with friendly fa[ces]
...with music thro[ugh]...
...to cool and...
...ers of field and...
...among the clove[r]
...en sweetness lu[...]
...of peace unend[ing]
...Thee, Lord, for [...]

BLESSING OF ST. HUBERT—Blessing of huntsmen and their hounds of the Oak Grove Hunt Club took place early this morning during a Thanksgiving service held at St. George's Episcopal Church, Germantown. This ancient custom, originally called the "blessing of hounds," is derived from the middle ages when the protection of the patron saint of the hunt, St. Hubert, was invoked at the beginning of a morning's sport. Rev. Charles E. Widney, rector of the church, is pictured surrounded by members of his

...ing for the service. The modern service, the rector's belief, in the words of the rector, that His creatures, both great and small, and that a good life should be the aim of men and women today." Special prayers of Thanksgiving were held after the service on the lawn of the church where the rector blessed the riders and their horses before they left to ride thru the lovely autumn countryside of Germantown, capped with...

Order of Service
For
THE ORDINATION TO THE PRIESTHOOD
of
The Reverend Robertson Eppes, Jr., B.D.
and
The Reverend Thomas Adams Roberts

SAINT MARY'S (GAILOR MEMORIAL) CATHEDRAL
Memphis, Tennessee

Saturday, Ember Day, February 28, 1953, 10 a.m.

●

The Right Reverend Edmund Pendleton Dandridge, D.D.
Bishop of Tennessee
The Right Reverend Theodore Nott Barth, D.D.
Bishop Coadjutor of Tennessee
Bishop's Chaplain and Magister: The Reverend Canon James Robert Sharp, D.D.
Preacher: The Reverend Donald Henning, D.D.
Presenting Priests: The Very Reverend William Evan Sanders, S.T.M.
and
The Reverend Eric Sutcliffe Greenwood, B.D.
Assisting Priests: The Reverend Robert Malcolm McNair, Ph.D.
The Reverend Wallace Morris Pennepacker, Th.B.
The Reverend St. Julian Aaron Simpkins, Jr., B.D.

●

(Page numbers refer to the Book of Common Prayer found in the pews)

Processional Hymn 220, "God of the Prophets"..................*L. Bourgeois*
Sermon
Reading of the Preface to the Ordinal (page 529)
Hymn 535, "Rise up, O Men of God"..................*Walker*
Presentation of the Candidates (page 536)
The Litany Hymn 332, "Saviour, When in Dust to Thee"..................*Carr*
(one verse)
The Litany for Ordinations (page 560)
Introit: "God Be In My Head"..................*Davies*
The Order for Holy Communion (page 67)
Kyrie Eleison (page 70)..................*Missa Marialis*
The Collect, Epistle, and Gospel (page 537)
The Examination and Ordination (pages 539-546)
The Nicene Creed (page 71)
The Offertory: "Jerusalem, O Turn Thee To The Lord" from GALLIA....*Gounod*
Prayer for the Whole State of Christ's Church (page 74)
Sanctus (page 77)..................*Missa Marialis*
Following the Prayer of Humble Access (page 82) shall be sung
Agnus Dei..................*Missa Marialis*
The Gloria in Excelsis (page 84)..................*Old Scottish Chant*
Collect and Benediction (page 547)
Recessional Hymn 256, "O Spirit of the Living God"..................*Webbe*

Mr. Douglas Barnett, Organist and Choirmaster

Once a Businessman, Now He Is a Minister

By THOMAS N. PAPPAS JR.
Press-Scimitar Staff Writer

And Businessmen Who Meet Him At Coffee Club Daily Get a Lift

Every morning between 8 and 9, Monday thru Saturday, they "settle the problems of the world" at Posey's Drug Store in Germantown.

"They" are the dozen or more Germantown business, civic and religious leaders who have an informal "Coffee Club" to which they repair for a bit of friendly fellowship and talk each day.

When the sessions are over, all take off for their day's work, somehow uplifted.

Among them is Tom Roberts, 35, who sort of bubbles over with enthusiasm and good nature. In other words, you like him the moment you meet him.

Roberts, rector of St. George's Episcopal Church at Germantown, thinks there should be more such "Coffee Clubs" in the various communities in and around Memphis.

"I know it has done much for me," he said, "in the way of getting to know people and sharing our friendship and neighborliness."

Big, friendly Tom Roberts used to be a businessman himself and when the early morning shop talk gets around to that or world affairs or any other subject he's in there holding up his end of the conversation.

Tom was quite a while coming around to the ministry, even tho both his grandfathers were ministers.

Native of Findlay, Ohio, everybody in his family sort of took it for granted he would become a minister.

Not so, Tom. He resisted it.

Studied for a year at Wittenberg College in Springfield, Ohio, then a year at Lafayette College at Easton, Pa.

Took a summer job with International Business Machines Corporation, then when they offered him a position in the sales department the accounting machine division took that.

He spent five years with I.B.M., 1938 to 1943, and was manager of their sub-offices at Knoxville and Johnson City.

Then he decided to strike out for himself, helped found the M. M. Hedges Manufacturing Co. at Chattanooga, of which he was vice president and general manager.

At a wedding in Knoxville, he met Miss Josephyne Turner Walton. They announced their engagement the week she reigned as

* * *

REV. THOMAS A. ROBERTS

queen of the Cotton Ball, Chattanooga's annual debutante affair. They were married, now have two children—Tommy, 10, and Jody, 7.

Tom thrived on business, enjoyed it, but inside something was growing.

As a layman, he took active part in the Church of the Good Shepherd on Lookout Mountain at Chattanooga.

Just as his family had expected all along, he turned to the ministry. Not a sudden thing at all.

But a gradual understanding of this: "I couldn't conscientiously do anything else."

He and Mrs. Roberts talked it over. She lent encouragement. He and Bishop Edmund P. Dandridge talked, too. More encouragement.

Tom enrolled at Sewanee, did his seminary work in stepped-up courses, was ordained a deacon by Bishop Theodore N. Barth Aug. 21, 1952, in Chattanooga, came to St. George's at Germantown, was ordained to the priesthood Feb. 28, 1953, becoming rector.

Since he has been there, a new church, new parish hall and rectory have been built, and there's 20 acres for future growth—perhaps for a recreational center and a school.

Six-three, weighing some 218 pounds, Tom Roberts used to play basketball and high jump a bit in high school. Resulted in two knee injuries, necessitating operations. He's O.K. now. In fact, in such good shape he's Civil Aeronautics Patrol chaplain, with the rank of lieutenant colonel.

Big grin, big booming voice, he's an important asset to that morning "Coffee Club" at Germantown.

Some months ago, while Mrs. Roberts was ill in a hospital following an operation, he stood facing the altar in St. George's Church conducting ante-communion and litany. When he faced the altar at the early morning service, only a few communicants were in the church.

When he turned back again, 14 members of the "Coffee Club"—many of whom are of other denominations—had walked in to attend his service.

It was their way of showing him that they, too, hoped Mrs. Roberts would soon be well.

And she was.

A HOME AND HOBBY SHOP will be converted into a church—this rectangular brick building will become the new home for St. George's Episcopal Church, Germantown.

Winston Home Purchased By St. George's Church

It's Being Converted Into Parish Hall, Church Building, and a Rectory

By CATHERINE MEACHAM, *Press-Scimitar Staff Writer*

St. George's Episcopal Church, Germantown, has bought the red brick home of Mr. and Mrs. Philip R. Winston near Germantown and the 19 acres of land surrounding the residence.

This home is being converted into a church building, parish hall and rectory for St. George's by Windrom of Northern & Windrom Architects.

In the transaction Mr. Winston obtained the present church building of white clapboard, built in Germantown in 1937.

The new church property faces Poplar Pike and backs on Dogwood Road. The present entrance road from Poplar will be curved to pass the building and around to the back. Parking areas will be on both the east and west sides.

The home, which Mr. Winston says was copied from a Virginia farm home, gives the appearance of a rectangular barn and was used not only as a home by the Winston family but as a hobby shop for Mr. Winston, who had woodworking and electronical equipment in one part of it.

Built of red brick on a concrete foundation, it has aluminum windows and slate roof. The rectory is in the Winston apartment which will be useless the rectory for Rev. and Mrs. Thomas A. Roberts. This apartment, paneled in solid mahogany and solid cypress, has a living room, dining room, three bedrooms, two tiled baths and a kitchen.

The east end of the building will be used as the church. This will be 36 by 40 feet and will seat 180 people. It will have a ceiling of exposed rafters and walls of veneer plywood.

A main entrance porch and doorway will be located in the center of the building facing Poplar. Here, the steeple will be erected. The doorway under the steeple will lead into a vestibule where a stairway will rise to the upper story and a 36 by 48 foot parish hall with adjoining kitchen and rest rooms. The fireplace, built by the Winstons for this room, which they planned to make into a recreation room, will be kept. The steeple tower will be covered with cypress siding to match the ends of the building.

Parishioners of St. George's are still worshipping in the old church in Germantown, but plans now are that the interior of the new church will be completed in time for them to move in by June 1. The steeple will be built later.

Announcement of the buying of this new property, made necessary by the growth of the church, is made by the rector, Mr. Roberts; the planning committee, Dunbar Abston and Winston Cheairs Jr.; the senior warden, Charles Kortrecht, and the junior warden, Pembroke Pinckney.

Also announced today is the opening of a campaign to raise $60,000 for the church building fund. The campaign will open Wednesday with a "kick-off" dinner at the new church building.

ST. GEORGE'S PLANS — A .... steeple .... be ... major change in the newly-....... property .. St. .....e's Episcopal Church in ......ntown. The church ex-.... to move into the con-.....ed laboratory-home by .... erecting the steeple ..... The 19-acre tract is . .....way 73 and Degroat ....

ST. GEORGE'S EPISCOPAL MISSION OFFICERS.

January 1, 1935.

Mr. John B. Scruggs, Lay Reader

Mr. J. B. Hebron, Sr. Warden

Mr. Carl Graves, Junior Warden

Mr. Joseph A. Martin, Secretary

Mr. Charles Speers, Treasurer

HISTORY OF THE GERMANTOWN COMMUNITY EPISCOPAL CHURCHES.

Mrs. Ellen Davies Rogers gives the following information on St. George's Episcopal Church of Germantown in her book, 'The Romance of the Episcopal Church in West Tennessee', published in 1964:

Church Name	Location	Date Originated	Date to Diocese
St. George	Germantown Shelby County	6/13/1934	1940

First Church House	First Rector	Present Rector
10/6/1936	Rev. Guy S. Usher 1940-1942 Rev. Charles Widney 1942-1952	David Babin 1962-

Church was named in memory of George Hanks and George Bennett, who died when small children, their parents were among the founders. Early ministers were: Sterling Tracy, Charles Seymour, Prentice Pugh, John Scruggs, Lay Reader, assisted. First services held in homes and in Presbyterian church. New church built on Poplar Pike, 1954. First church building presently used as Germantown Library. Church began with 17 communicants; at present over 200 adult members.

After much research, such as personal interviews with some of the elder residents of Germantown and with one of the charter members of St. George's mission, and from information from old records, I believe that part of the above information was actually in reference to an Episcopal Church in the Germantown community in the 1800's rather than to that of St. George's church of Germantown. The first Episcopal church, located at the corner of Old Poplar Pike and Kirby Road had no connection with the present St. George's church; it having been torn down long before the 1900's. This first Episcopal church was possibly named for the children, George Hanks and George Bennett, who died as small children, as it is believed their parents were among the founders of that church. It is a fact that they were not members of St. George's in Germantown as they were deceased long before it was founded. It is also believed that the Rev. Charles Seymour may have been a minister at that church as there is no memory of him by one of the founders of St. George's who came here in 1918. She does remember the Rev. Prentice Pugh as having been an Episcopal minister who held services at the Germantown Presbyterian church once a month before St. George's mission was founded.

The Germantown communicants met in private home before the organization of the mission in 1934. Shortly after St. George's Mission was organized, the use of the lower floor of the Germantown Masonic building was secured as a meeting place for the mission's communicants.

Shortly after his ordination, the Rev. Sterling Tracy was in charge of the pastoral care of the mission for a short while...the exact dates not available. He was succeeded by the Rev. Guy S. Usher...1940-1942; the Rev. Charles Widney...1942-1952; the Rev. Thomas A. Roberts...1952-1956; the Rev. Frank M. McClain...1957-1961; and the Rev. David E. Babin...1962-   , present rector.

When Archdeacor Charles W. Weller first mentioned the unused lot at the northwest corner of Germantown Road and West Street to Mr. John Scruggs and the idea of forming a mission was suggested, there were only 10 adult communicants attending meetings in the community and they told Mr. Scruggs they doubted it it were possible to establish a mission at that time. However, Mr. Scruggs refused to listen to their doubts and they decided to help him attain his dream it at all possible. These communicants were: Mr. John Scruggs, Mr. J. B. Hebron,

Mr. and Mrs. Carl Graves; Mr. and Mrs. Hiram T. Adair; Mrs. Joe B. Kirby; Mrs. Mamie Cloyes; and Mr. and Mrs. Joseph A. Martin, in whose home the first meeting for the purpose of organizing a mission was held in June, 1934. These same 10 communicants were the founders of St. George's Episcopal Mission and the signers of the first petition. The Messers: John B. Scruggs; J. B. Hebron; Joseph A. Martin, and Charles Speers were appointed to the Bishop's Committee, January 1, 1935. It might be noted that when the first meeting was held Mr. and Mrs. Speers were not communicants of Germantown as they were attending a church in Memphis at the time.

The first services of the mission were held in the Masonic building on Sunday, June 17, 1934, with the Sacrements of Holy Communion being celebrated by the Rev. Charles W. Weller, assisted by Mr. John Scruggs, Lay Reader. Services continued there each Sunday thereafter for approximately 3 years with Mr. Scruggs presiding, except for the 3rd Sunday of each month when Archdeacon Weller celebrated with the Sacraments of Holy Communion.

A branch of the Ladies' Auxiliary was organized shortly; and, they, the congregation, and the church officers began working to raise funds to build a chapel on the lot across the street. Through the generous respons of individuals, other churches, and the Church Extension Fund of New York, they were soon successful.

Services commemorating the laying of the corner stone were held October 11, 1936, with Archdeacon Weller presiding. Official papers of the church and of the Diocese, a short history of the mission, and a list of the approximately 100 people attending the services were deposited in the copper lined cornerstone. The previous Saturday,

Archdeacon Weller had announced his retirement, effective January 1, 1937, and had expressed his hopes that the chapel building would be completed in December and his presiding over the dedication services would be his last official act before his retirement. However, the chapel was not completed until later in the spring and he was unable to attend at the time. However he did visit the chapel shortlt afterwards. Dedication services were held on Easter Sunday, March 17, 1937, at 4:00 P.M., by Bishop Maxon, assisted by a number of Memphis clergy. St. John's of Memphis furnished a choir for the occasion.

St. George's church family grew rapidly and in 1940 it was admitted to the Dioscese as a church and no longer a mission. When one stops to think that the economical structure of the country in the late 1930's was not a time of great prosperity as it is today, it is amasing that all these developements were accomplished in only 6 years; and, the chapel building was completely free of debt when completed.

I'm not sure of the exact date, but it was during the early 1940's that the property at 2602 South Germantown Rd. was purchased and the residence was used as a rectory....that was before there were any house numbers in the county. The church school membership had grown so rapidly that it had become necessary that class rooms be built. Class rooms were built on the north end of the church building.

The church family continued to grow so rapidly that it was becoming impossible to seat them for Sunday services. Everyone realized something had to be done...but what? There was no room left for enlarging the present building; yet, the family disliked the idea of having to leave its beautiful little clapboard home. However, in 1953, it bought the red brick home of Mr. and Mrs. Phillip B. Winston and the 20 acres of ground surrounding the residence on Highway #72 East of Germantown, Mr. and Mrs. Winston obtained the white clapboard home of St. George's family and the rectory in the transaction. Later the church building were sold by the Winstons for use as a library.

The Winston residence, copied from a Virginia farm home, gave the appearance of a rectangular barn and was used as both a home and as a hobby shop for Mr. Winston, who had wood working and electronical equipment in one part of it. Built of red brick on a concrete foundation, it had aluminium windows and a gabled roof. On the west end was the Winston apartment paneled in solid mahogany and solid cypress. This apartment was converted into a rectory after it was purchased by St. George's family.

The east end of the building was converted into a church 36 feet x 40 feet to seat 180 people. It had a high ceiling with exposed rafters. The east walls were paneled in veneer plywood with a matching natural wood cross hung above the altar. A main entrance to the church and a steeple tower were erected on the couth side facing the highway. The steeple tower was covered with cypress siding to match the ends of the building. The doorway under the steeple lead to a vestibule with entrances to the church and to the rectory. A stairway at the west end of the church lead to the upper story where there was a 36 feet x 48 feet parish hall which was used for church school class rooms on Sundays. Portable partitions were used to divide the hall into class rooms.

A ground breaking ceremony was held June 26, 1961, on a site just northeast of the church building where St. George's Day School was to be built. It was also to be used for church school class rooms. The day school is a private school for elementary pupils that began its first year with a kindergarten and one grade. A grade a year is being added until it will have six grades and a kindergarten.

The fall of 1964 saw a new brick rectory completed at 8251 Dogwood Road.

St. George's communicants numbered 261 as of December 31, 1964. Out of the original 10 communicants of St. George's Mission there is only 1 communicant still in our family of today....7 having moved from the community and transfered out; the other two are deceased. The original 25 or so families represented when St. George's chapel was built have moved away over the past 30 years and have left only about half of these families still represented in our church family today. Our family is steadily growing and it is hoped that, although we were unable to say our new home, rectory and school are free of debt, that some of us who had the privelege of moving into our first church family free of debt will also one day before too many years see our second home completely free of debt.

DOCUMENT 15

History

St. George's Mission held its first service on Sunday, June 17, 1934, meeting in the Germantown Masonic Hall. On October 11, 1936, the cornerstone of a new church was laid and the finished building was consecrated by Bishop Maxon on March 17, 1937. The site had been given to the diocese of Tennessee some 50 years earlier by a Mr. Botts of Olive Branch, Mississippi. This building, depicted above, became the Germantown City Library, after the congregation moved to its present site. In 1969, the Germantown Presbyterian Church bought the building for use as a chapel. The house behind the Masonic Hall, now 2402 Germantown Road, was the rectory prior to the move.

The Mission progressed steadily until, in 1940, it became a parish. Then, in April 1953, the congregation purchased the home and hobby shop of Mr. and Mrs. Philip B. Winston, together with 19 acres, on Highway 72. With suitable conversion, the hobby shop end of the building became the church and the home became the rectory. To some in the still small congregation, this all seemed a lot to take on , but subsequent growth proved it right.

The next major development was the starting of a Day School in the fall of 1959, meeting in the church and in the 'little red school house', otherwise known as the 'chicken coop'. In June, 1961, work began on a six-classroom addition. In 1964 we built a fine new rectory on Dogwood Road. In 1966 we were able to convert the former rectory into Church offices, choir rooms and an enlarged church, including a balcony. Then, in 1967, we began work on a parish hall/gymnasium, together with two large classrooms and in 1970, our Day School, now grown to 140 pupils, conducted its own fund raising drive and started construction of a new six-classroom addition to double the capacity of the school, kindergarten through sixth grade. During these years, the parish also grew to 500 communicants, plus a hundred or more baptized members.

Records of clergy in the early days are somewhat scant, but we know that the Rev. Sterling Tracy was in charge at first, and that later clergy, with dates, were the Rev. Guy S. Usher, 1940-42; the Rev. Charles L. Widney, 1942-52; the Rev. Thomas S. Roberts, 1952-56; the Rev. Frank M. McLain, 1957-61; the Rev. David E. Babin, 1962-65; the Rev. Robert M. Cherry, 1965-67; the Rev. Sidney G. Ellis from 1967.

With the enormous housing expansion in the Germantown area since 1968, it is apparent that the future of St. George's Church and School is very encouraging and with God's blessing, we shall go far.

DOCUMENT 16

St. George's Episcopal Church

St. George's Episcopal Church

In the early 1800's the Episcopal communicants of the community met in private homes and occasionally in a Presbyterian Church located at the corner of Poplar Pike and Kirby Rd. In the early 1900's the same was true except they met once a month for services in the Germantown Presbyterian Church, the other building having been torn down.

The later part of the 1800's a lot at the northwest corner of Germantown d. and West St., was given to the Diocese of Tenn., by a Mr. Betts of Olive Branch, Miss., on which to build a chapel building when it was needed. This lot went unused and almost unforgotten for the next 30 years or so.

June 1, 1934 a petition to the Diocese of Tenn., for a chapel was signed by 10 communicants of the community and sent to Bishop Maxon who accepted it and appointed a Bishop's Committee.

The Committee became active at once and secured the use of the lower floor of the Germantown Lodge building as a meeting place.

The first official service was held there on Sunday, June 17, 1934 and continued there until the spring of 1937 and church school classes continued to meet at the Lodge building until class rooms were added to the church building several years later.

The church officers and congregation began plans for a chapel and were soon successful. Ground was laid on Oct. 8, 19__. The building was erected in the spring of 19__ and dedication and Consecration services were held on _____, ____, 19__.

ware on the doors was furnished by a friend in whose family it had been for some 50 years. A giant oak tree, possibly 50 years old, at the _____ built _____ en _____ the _____ beautiful Chapel. This beauty was later further enhanced by ivy from cuttings, secured by special permission from the historical Westminister Abbey of London, England.

The interior of the chapel was unique. The walls were covered with richly grained plywood finished with cherry shellac. The windows were hand grained. The beautiful hand finished pews, of the early church design, bore beautiful brass name plates. The Altar, the Lectern, Altar rail, etc., were hand made and finished to blend with the interior design. A beautiful round memorial window picturing the Virgin and Child was placed in the north wall directly over the Altar. Electric lights, resembling old time kerosene lamps, were hung in clusters of three from the large wood beams in the high ceiling. Gas floor furnaces furnished heat.

St. George's family continued to grow, class rooms were added on the north end of the chapel. In 1940 it was admitted to the Diocese as a parish church and a home was purchased for the Rector at ____ S. Germantown _____ The continued growth of church family and lack of any available building space in the ground made _____ and there _____ at ____ S. _____ It was purchased by _____ Church and the _____

Virginia farm home, gave the appearance of a rectangular barn, and had been used as a residence and hobby shop. The west end was converted into a rectory. It was paneled in solid mahogany and solid cypress. The east end was converted into a church 36' x 40'. It had high exposed rafters. Natural veneer plywood paneling on the east wall, a natural wood cross, natural wood furnishings, pews, etc., were added. A main entrance to the church and a steeple tower were erected on the south side of the building. The steeple tower was covered with cypress siding to match the ends of the building. The doorway under the steeple led to a vestibule (Narthex) with entrances to the church and to the church offices. A stairway at the west end of the church led up the 36' x 48' parish hall which was used for class rooms.

The fall of 1959, St. George's Day School opened with a kindergarten class and 1 grade. The parish house was used for the school's temporary quarters, the Rector having moved to temporary quarters in the Nursery building. The new Day School building and Parish house was completed in 1962. One grade has been added each year bringing the school to _ Kindergarten and 6 grades.

The fall of 1964 brought the completion of a new two story brick home for the Rector at 2251 Dogwood Rd.

St. George's Episcopal Church, its new Rector, the Rev. Robert Cherry, Mrs. Cherry and their four children _____ other churches _____

dent of the community as well as a cordial invitation to join in the church services.

ST. GEORGE'S SCHEDULE
During the month of Aug. only two Sunday morning services are being held at 7:30 A.M. and at 10:00 A.M.
Beginning Sept. 5th, the following schedule:
SUNDAYS: 7:30 a.m. — Holy Communion.
9:15 a.m. — Church School and Service.
11:00 a.m. — Morning Prayer or Holy Communion.
MID-WEEK: 10:00 a.m. Holy Communion on Wednesdays, Fridays and Holy Days.

DOCUMENT 17
ST. GEORGE'S EPISCOPAL CHURCH
GERMANTOWN, TENNESSEE

The Reverend
Thomas Adams Roberts
Rector

November 21, 1955

Ladies and Gentlemen:

Interest in Saint George's Church has been shown by communicants in many ways and yet there are some who have only a limited knowledge of Church history, progress made in the last few years, or activities of today.

Knowing that a well informed Church family bespeaks for pride and satisfaction in our religious affiliations, the Vestry are undertaking, through this and a subsequent letter, to give you a word picture of Saint George's of yesterday and of today.

Since her humble beginning as a Mission in June of 1934, with a charter membership of ten, Saint George's Church has weathered and overcome hardships that, in retrospect, would seem to deserve commendation. In January 1944 Saint George's Church was admitted by the Convention of the Diocese of Tennessee to full Parish status and today . . . with a total Church family of 252 and an attendance record that compares most favorably with that of the other Churches in the surrounding area . . . she is an integral part of community spiritual education and well being.

Saint George's Church perhaps exceeds neighboring Churches in number of worship services held. We have maintained an average of five per week, not including special Lenten services and on Holy Days. Attendance at Sunday services has averaged 160.

Through a most ambitious program, Saint George's acquired our present Church, Parish House and Rectory, with surrounding twenty acres of land, the value of which is conservatively estimated at $90,000.00. These enlarged facilities were financed by the sale of the former Church property, a bank loan, through membership gifts and pledges for future payment. In less than three years we have achieved substantial remodeling to Church and Rectory, new Sunday School equipment, new driveways, grading and sodding of grounds, air conditioning equipment, new organ and many other items. Remaining obligations include balance on long term mortgage and on bank loans of less than $25,000.00 combined total, from which pledges for future payment, already received, may be deducted. A truly remarkable achievement.

Progress to date seems to portend continued rapid expansion. In fact, already Sunday School facilities are inadequate. It is commonly felt that planning for further expansion is fully justified and necessary. We will welcome your interest and support, as we believe that every communicant of Saint George's Church will receive spiritual recompense and justifiable pride in proportion to your knowledge of and participation in the affairs of Saint George's Church in the future.

Later this week we shall send you a suggested plan for personal participation in the current operating budget. We shall give, for your consideration, information about the very real current problems of a Church that no longer can be viewed as a little operation, but, instead, one which has taken her place as a vital member in the Diocese, the nation and the world, and one deserving the support of all Episcopalians in our progressive community.

Among our daily blessings, let's not overlook and fail to give thanks for Saint George's and the opportunity for social, spiritual and religious growth afforded through the revitalized Parish Family.

                                                              Sincerely yours,

                                                                  The Vestry

Index

A.

Abednego, 79
Abston, Dunbar, 106
Acklen, John,
Acklen, Louise Finley, 13, 19, 60
Adair, Hiram, 37, 38, 39, 45 62, 72, 74
Adair, Lotta, 3, 7, 16, 18, 20, 37
Anderson, Mary May, 4
Ave Maria Home, 51

B.

Babin, David, E., 117, 118
Bailey's Station, Tennessee, 2
Baptists, 1
Bedford, Helen Mangrum
Bennett Family, 3, 17
Bennett, George, 13
Bledsoe, Steve, 117
Blount, John, 11
Bott, W. W., 10, 70
Brookhaven Cumberland Presbyterian Church, 14
Brooks, Joseph, 14
Brooks, Wilks, 46
Bruce, Ben Mrs. , 17, 75
Buckingham, H. E., 75
Butterworth, Frances (See Frances Martin)

C.

Calvary Episcopal Church, 34, 38, 41, 54, 73, 93
Cannon, Devereaux Mrs., 39
Catholic Church, 29
Catmur, Eric, 117
Catmur, Margaret, 117
Central High School, 41
Chambers, Arthur B., 8, 17
Charlotte, North Carolina, 51
Cherry, Robert, 118
Chicago, Illinois, 54, 58
Church of the Good Shepherd, 75, 85
Church of the Advent, 9

C., Continued

Closter, Mary Hayes Willis, 4
Cloyes, Harry, 52
Cloyes, Mamie, 51, 52, 53, 54, 75
Collierville, Tennessee, 1, 7, 20, 25, 59, 83
Columbia Institute, 44
Columbia, South Carolina, 118
Columbia, Tennessee, 44
Cooke, C. Allen, 120, 121, 122
Coppock, Paul, 1
Cowan, Joan, 117
Crook, Jere, 93
Cubine, James W., 122, 123
Cumberland Presbyterian Church, 14, 15

D.

Dakin, W. E., 69
Dean, Dennis, 106
Dent, Lucian Minor, 66
DeSoto County, Mississippi, 10
Diocese of West Tennessee, 123, 125
Dixon, Alex D., 123
Dodge, Elizabeth, 54

E.

Ellis, Sidney G., 119
Elwood Cemetery, 47, 54
Emmanuel Church, LaGrange, 4
Episcopal Church Extension Fund, 67

F.

Finley, Louise (See Louise Acklen)
Finley, Roy Mark, 72, 74
Firestone, Raymond C., 95
Fox, George, 16

G.

Gailor, Thomas F., 4, 5, 7
Germantown Baptist Church, 1, 15, 30, 45

G., Continued

Germantown F & AM Lodge No. 95 (Masonic Lodge Hall), 12, 26, 63, 64, 65, 69, 77, 78, 91, 92
Germantown Methodist Church, 5
Germantown Presbyterian Church, 7, 8, 18, 19, 76, 123
Germantown Road, 70, 92
Germantown, Tennessee, 1, 2, 3, 4, 7, 9, 12, 18, 25, 28, 32, 34, 78, 124
Gibson, George Calvin, 121, 122
Gloster, Mary Hayes Willis, 4
Grace Episcopal Church, 44, 49, 75
Grace-St. Luke's Episcopal Church, 43, 51
Grant, U. S., 32
Graves, Carl Richmond, 40, 41, 42, 62, 82
Graves, Mary Ellen, 40, 41, 42
Greenville, Mississippi, 27, 33, 41
Greenville, South Carolina, 116

H.

Hammond, James, 70, 89
Hanks, 3, 17, 76
Hanks, George, 13, 18
Harriman, Tennessee, 116
Hebron, John Bell, 31, 32, 33, 42, 62, 63, 65, 72, 74, 82
Hebron, Nanie B., 34
Holy Trinity Episcopal Chruch, 7, 8, 9

K.

King, Frank Sr., 95
Kirby, Dorothy W., 21, 43, 44, 45, 46, 47
Kirby, Joseph Brooks, 44, 46
Kirby, Louise Ann, 44
Knoxville, Tennessee, 45, 47
Kortrecht, Charles, 96

L.

LaGrange, Tennessee, 4
Lancers, 120

M.

Martin, Frances, 48, 49
Martin, Geraldine Apperson, 48, 61, 67
Martin, Joseph Abram, 48, 61, 62, 67
Martin, Joseph Junior, 49
Martindale, 49, 67
Maryville, Tennessee,
Masonic Lodge Hall, see Germantown F & AM Lodge No. 95
Maury, Poston W., 10
Maxon, James, 11, 32, 55, 72, 75, 80
McClain, Frank M., 115, 116, 117, 118
Memphis Press-Scimitar, 48
Meshack, 79
Messicks, 3, 7, 17
Methodists, 1
Mimosa, 70, 89
Moore, William R. Dry Goods Co., 57

N.

New York Giants Baseball Club, 77
Noe, Israel H., 9

O.

O'Brien, James W., 96
O'Neil, Arthur, 28
O'Neil, Nellie Conn, 28
O'Neil, Nellie Pearl, 28, 29
Otey Memorial Chapel, 87

P.

Presbyterians, 1
Pugh, Prentice, 6, 7, 8, 9

Q.

Quintard, Charles T., 1

R.

Roberts, Thomas A., 97, 98, 100, 104, 106, 116
Rogers, Ellen Davies, 13
Rose, David, 81
Rosengarten, Louise (See Acklen, Louise)

S.

Sanders, William E., 121
Scruggs, John Bridges, 24, 25, 26, 27, 28, 29, 33, 59, 62, 63, 64, 69, 74, 79
Scruggs, Pearl O'Neil, 28, 29, 30
Sewanee, Tennessee, 87
Shadrach, 79
Shelby, Isaac, 56
Shepherd, S. J., 10, 11
Simpson, Thomas, 81
Sloan, Paul E., 90
Smith, Mrs. Clarence, 1
Speer, Charles E., 21, 54, 55, 56, 62, 63
Speer, Elizabeth, 21, 54, 55, 56
Spring Street, Germantown, 70
Stillwell, Laura, 3
Strickland Family, 11, 12, 70
St. Andrews, Collierville, 2, 7, 20, 25, 59, 83, 85, 91
St. Andrews, Maryville, Tennessee, 120
St. Ann's, Woodstock, 83, 85, 91
St. George's Day School, 117, 119
St. James Episcopal, Greenville, Mississippi, 33
St. John's Episcopal Church, Knoxville, 117
St. John's Episcopal Church, Memphis, 69
St. Mary's Catholic Church, 29
St. Matthew's, Covington, 124
Strong, Ada, 58
Steuterman, A., 73
Sweetbriar College, 117

T.

Terry, William (Memphis Bill), 77
Tracy, Sterling, 73, 80
Twyford, William, 29

U.

Usher, Guy S., 81, 82, 84, 85, 86, 88

V.

von Arx, Marie Theresia (See Mamie Cloyes)

W.

Walker, Olive B., 44
Walker, Richard Gordon, 44
Weller, Charles K., 25, 49, 59, 69, 73, 79
West, Betsy, 5
Widney, Charles L., 86, 87, 89, 90
Williamson, Edwin S., 9, 21, 23, 56, 57, 58
Williamson, Laura Lee, 9
Wills, Dorothy K., 44, 45, 46
Wills, Walter, 45
Wilson, Mark K., 124
Winston, Phillip, 100, 104
Winston, Virginia, 104
Woodruff, William E., 48

Y.

Yancey, Edwin T., Senior (II), 3, 4, 9, 10, 20, 38, 59
Yancey Family, 3, 17

Z.

Zook, Morgan Mrs., 39